The Food of
SICILY

The Food of
SICILY

Recipes from a Sun-Drenched
Culinary Crossroads

FABRIZIA LANZA

WITH KATE WINSLOW

Photographs by Guy Ambrosino

ARTISAN BOOKS

NEW YORK

Library of Congress Cataloging-in-Publication Data

Names: Lanza, Fabrizia, author. | Winslow, Kate, author. | Ambrosino, Guy, photographer.
Title: The food of Sicily / Fabrizia Lanza with Kate Winslow ; photographs by Guy Ambrosino.
Description: New York : Artisan Books, 2023 | Includes index.
Identifiers: LCCN 2022055231 | ISBN 9781579659868 (hardcover)
Subjects: LCSH: Cooking, Italian—Sicilian style. | LCGFT: Cookbooks.
Classification: LCC TX723.2.S55 L3543 2023 | DDC 641.59458—dc23/eng/20221122
LC record available at https://lccn.loc.gov/2022055231

Design by Jan Derevjanik

Artisan books are available at special discounts when purchased in bulk for premiums and sales promotions as well as for fundraising or educational use. Special editions or book excerpts can also be created to specification. For details, please contact special.markets@hbgusa.com.

The Hachette Speakers Bureau provides a wide range of authors for speaking events. To find out more, go to hachettespeakersbureau.com or email HachetteSpeakers@hbgusa.com.

Published by Artisan,
an imprint of Workman Publishing Co., Inc.,
a subsidiary of Hachette Book Group, Inc.
1290 Avenue of the Americas
New York, NY 10104
artisanbooks.com

Artisan is a registered trademark of Workman Publishing Co., Inc.,
a subsidiary of Hachette Book Group, Inc.

Printed in China on responsibly sourced paper
First printing, August 2023

10 9 8 7 6 5 4 3 2 1

For all who seek something
more than food in food

CONTENTS

INTRODUCTION

Sicily is the largest island in the Mediterranean, with a history that goes back millennia. It is speckled with ancient ruins, exceptional beaches, and ever-changing landscapes. Over the past few centuries, an abundance of native ingredients, both wild and farmed, has produced a cuisine that is renowned around the world. All of those factors, as well as the incredible warmth of its inhabitants, have turned this island into a magical place to explore. And yet, anyone who visits senses immediately that Sicily is a different world, in many ways still lost in time and secretive. You need to dig in a bit deeper to appreciate the real soul of this place.

My family has lived in Sicily for hundreds of years, owning large farms and vineyards, but I personally spent much of my adulthood in Northern Italy before returning to the island full-time some twenty years ago. People often ask me if I feel more Sicilian or Italian, and I find it a difficult question to answer. Of course, I am Italian, since Italy was united as a country in 1861, but a voice inside me proclaims, "I am Sicilian,

too!" I believe most Sicilians feel this way. Just a narrow strait divides Sicily from the mainland, but it certainly feels a world away. Because of our geography and history, we are both part of Italy and separate from it. We treasure our uniqueness from the rest of Italy while also feeling neglected by the mainland—outsiders in our own country. Sicily is on the edge, geographically and psychically, floating between Western Europe and the Middle East. Sicily is an island apart.

But this feeling of separation that Sicilians share does not mean we are all united. Indeed, there is no one Sicily. And you can see that first and foremost in the landscape. The rocky coastlines that give way to long beaches, the turquoise tropical waters, and the beautiful sunsets—these are some of the views you expect to see on an island in the middle of the Mediterranean. But then you bump into the tall, rugged mountains that run along the northern coast, offering dramatic vistas and drastic changes in weather and temperature. As you climb, the warmth of the seaside towns can give way to shade, fog, and cooler air that can drop below freezing at night in winter. Moving out of the mountains and following twisting, narrow roads into the interior of

OPPOSITE: *The morning sun shines over the daily market in the Piazza Carlo Alberto in Catania.*

Sicily, you are greeted by wide, hilly plains devoid of trees and sometimes seemingly of human life. Historically, it was difficult to travel from one part of the island to another (honestly, it is still a challenge), so people tended to stay in their little towns, from which all sorts of rituals and customs grew.

That diversity of landscape means there is also incredible biodiversity. Different types of soils and climates, combined with the fact that Sicily has, for centuries, been at the crossroads of one of the busiest trade routes of all time, have produced an amazing variety of both farmed crops and wild plants. So many delicious things grow here: olives, grapes, wheat, and all kinds of citrus, as well as dense, pulpy tomatoes, eggplant, peppers, and squash. This is why, despite centuries of poverty, a Sicilian could always eat well, even if it was only a slice of tomato and a salted sardine on a hunk of bread. A slight slowdown occurs in the growing season between December and January, but still you will see markets full of local artichokes, cauliflower, cardoons, broccoli, and heaps of wild fennel. Increasingly, you will find large orchards of avocados, mangoes, papaya, and lychees, transplants from the Far East or Africa, growing next to the tangerines and loquats that have been there for decades.

Where does Sicilian cooking stand in all of this? Is the common narrative depicting Sicily as a melting pot—a combination of cultural layers from the Greeks, Romans, Arabs, Normans, Spanish, and French who ruled our island at various times in history—still the best way to make sense of the complexity and richness of our food? Where does one find the real Sicilian cooking—in the many Michelin-starred restaurants scattered around the island, in its thousands of rosticcerie and street food stalls, or in the homes of the nonnas and other home cooks? What are the everyday eating habits of today's Sicilians? And what "Sicilians" are we talking about, anyway? Those living in the country, close to the land, or those who make their homes in the large cities? How many still have access to a real tomato grown in a nearby garden rather than in a who-knows-where greenhouse?

Not all of these questions can be addressed in one book, but you will find many answers in this collection of Sicilian recipes. Here you will find recipes for traditional classics such as pasta alla Norma, cannoli, and the Palermitan pizza known as sfincione, alongside more modern adaptations such as zucchini carpaccio and mackerel confit. Read the headnotes and you'll learn about the influences, adaptations, and new and old ways of cooking a recipe, for there is nothing more volatile in Sicily and elsewhere than a food "tradition." A recipe, beyond its deliciousness, can tell us a lot about the habits, lifestyle, culture, superstitions, and passions of a country. Of course, there are specific ways of doing things in Sicily, but as is the case anywhere else, those ways are constantly and continuously evolving, affected by moods, movements, challenges, economics, and so much more. The best thing to do is ask a lot of questions and pay endless, caring attention to what is happening around us—to be a hungry anthropologist!

As fertile as Sicily is, the Mediterranean diet and lifestyle championed by Ancel Keys after World War II—based on whole grains, legumes, lots of fruits and vegetables, and

OPPOSITE, CLOCKWISE: *Grapevines flourishing outside Alcamo; open-air newsstands dot the streets of Sicily's larger cities; from the beach in Mondello; a rosticceria's selection of pizzas and breads; the black pigs of the Nebrodi Mountains; the Santa Maria Assunta church in the town of Randazzo; small vegetable stands are a common sight all over the island.*

very little animal meat—is no longer the norm across the island. We may be an island apart, but that doesn't mean we're immune to the pitfalls of modern life. But on the flip side, the appreciation of organic farming and the acceptance of the Slow Food movement's tenets are now well supported by both chefs and the hundreds of small producers and farmers who have repopulated the island's interior.

Sicily's food traditions today are much less rooted in the religious calendar that once dictated life in many small villages, with feast days punctuating a life of scarcity and hardship. Now that everyone is more or less well-fed, food no longer has the symbolic relevance it once did. For example, cassata—an elaborate cake filled with sweetened ricotta and decorated with marzipan and a colorful assortment of candied fruits—was once solely eaten for Easter but is now available in pastry shops all year round. Fruits and vegetables that once belonged to specific seasons can be purchased at the supermarket at any time. Despite all of this, food remains for Sicilians a mark of pride and identity, the start of millions of endless discussions. And this book is the beginning of a voyage through Sicily with a different eye, one that is willing to go deeper than the usual accepted stories.

From my vantage point—running the cooking school that my mother, Anna Tasca Lanza, started some thirty-five years ago in a most remote and ancient part of Sicily—I have had the unique opportunity to encounter an incredible array of recipes and

traditions shared by both chefs and home cooks, farmers and aristocrats, shepherds and winemakers. I have experienced firsthand the variety and breadth of Sicilian food culture. There are different levels to understanding Sicilian cuisine— most notably, the broader, more regional perspective that offers lots of variability across the island and a hyperlocal one that is tied strongly to a sense of belonging to one certain place above all others.

Here you can find nearly as many caponata recipes as there are Sicilians. Likewise, every village, and every household within that village, will have its own recipe for tomato sauce. Some add sugar, some season with lots of basil, and others use only bay leaves, and quantities of onions and garlic can vary drastically—but usually the sauces are all outstandingly good, especially since the raw ingredients are stellar, so it all comes down to a matter of taste. At the other end of the spectrum, you will find couscous only on the western side of the island; it simply doesn't exist in Catania or Messina or Noto. Wild greens that are foraged and cherished in central Sicily are overlooked elsewhere, which confirms the concept that food is not just fuel but also a matter of choice and culture.

Writing an encyclopedia of Sicilian cuisine is impossible. It is too vast, varied, particular, and always on the move, like any lively food scene should be! This book's collection of recipes and history is meant to give you a taste of the island—to offer insight into how Sicilians feel about their ingredients and traditions, their ways of cooking, and today's eating habits. As these recipes come to life in your own kitchen, I hope that you get a sense of just how special Sicily is.

OPPOSITE: *The busy, colorful fish market in Catania is a feast for all senses.*

FOLLOWING PAGE: *A casual lunch of Sardines Stuffed with Bread Crumbs and Raisins (page 133), Mussel Gratin (page 34), and Citrus Risotto (page 123), accompanied by slices of semolina bread.*

STARTERS

antipasti

CHICKPEA FRITTERS 22
panelle

DEEP-FRIED RICE BALLS 24
arancine

RICOTTA FRITTERS 29
ricotta fritta

FRIED SEAFOOD 33
fritto misto di pesce

MUSSEL GRATIN 34
gratin di cozze

OCTOPUS SALAD 37
insalata di polipo

CITRUS-MARINATED SARDINES 40
sarde marinate

SAUTÉED BLACK OLIVES 41
olive nere saltate

GREEN OLIVE SALAD 43
insalata di olive verdi

ARTICHOKES PRESERVED IN OIL 49
carciofi sott'olio

Since the sixteenth century, small bites of cold food, called antipasto, have been served as part of an Italian meal as a way to awaken the appetite and prepare the stomach for the rest of the meal. These salads, charcuterie, olives, and pickles, known as servizi di credenza, could be prepared and set out in advance. During the nineteenth century, upper-class meals shifted away from the custom of laying all the foods out at the same time to dividing the meal into three or four courses, which included an antipasto, followed by a primo (generally pasta or soup), a secondo (meat or fish), dessert, and fruit.

In Sicily, proper antipasti were rarely part of an everyday meal for most people, belonging instead to the big ceremonial feasts that commemorated special occasions such as weddings and baptisms. However, in the streets of Palermo and Catania, you could easily find small bites and casual snacks. Called in Sicilian dialect *grape u' pitittu* ("open the appetite"), these could be dishes of mussels, sea urchins, or octopus; the chickpea fritters called panelle; potato croquettes; or small chunks of boiled meats—anything from the pig's head to its chewy, cartilaginous feet, sprinkled with salt and lemon juice—that one ate standing in the street.

Restaurants and trattorias fancied the upper-class tradition of offering many small plates of charcuterie and pickles and started to make it their own. Today, many popular restaurants in Sicily will have near the entrance a large table draped in a white cloth and covered with all sorts of antipasti and pickles where customers can serve themselves. The selection will almost certainly include fried food, such as fried ricotta, and various iterations of marinated or raw fish—the crudo that has become very fashionable in the last two decades—as well as fish salads, wedges of frittata, caponata, tangy preserved artichokes or eggplants, and other vegetables. Likewise, Sicilian home cooks happily juggle making briny olive salads, arancine, and fritto misto in their own kitchens. The idea is the same as in the old days: The antipasti, mostly served at room temperature and often brightly seasoned with vinegar or lemon, are meant to welcome you to the table and warm up your appetite before the big meal.

CHICKPEA FRITTERS

panelle

SERVES 10

2½ cups (250 g) finely ground chickpea flour (see Resources, page 310)

3 cups plus 2 tablespoons (750 ml) cold water

Fine sea salt and freshly ground black pepper

Vegetable oil, for frying

A panini of chickpea fritters and potato crocché sandwiched into a white bread roll called mafalda is a classic street food in Palermo. Sold from street stalls in the city's old sections, it is a filling meal that both workers and students enjoy. The recipe for panelle consists of just two ingredients—very finely ground chickpea flour and water—that are cooked together like polenta. The resulting mixture is spread out into a thin layer, cooled, and then cut into smaller pieces and deep-fried until golden and crisp. Served with a glass of white wine, panelle make a very refined appetizer.

IN A MEDIUM saucepan, combine the chickpea flour, water, and a pinch each of salt and pepper and whisk until smooth. Cook over medium-high heat, whisking constantly, until the mixture is like a very stiff polenta, about 8 minutes. (Reduce the heat if necessary to keep it from burning.) Switch to stirring with a wooden spoon and cook, stirring constantly, until the mixture pulls away from the sides of the pan, about 3 minutes. Working quickly, transfer the hot mixture to three or four large plates and use an offset spatula to spread it out to about ¼ inch (6 mm) thick. (Alternatively, spread it out to ¼ inch/6 mm on one large baking sheet.) Let cool to room temperature, 15 to 20 minutes.

Loosen the edges of the cooled panelle mixture with a knife. Carefully peel the pieces of dough off the plates and place them on a clean work surface, stacking one on top of the other. Cut the stack into 16 equal wedges. (If using a baking sheet, cut the dough into 2-inch/5 cm squares.)

Pour at least 2 inches (5 cm) of vegetable oil into a wide heavy-bottomed pot and heat over medium-high heat until it is hot enough to fry in (see Deep-Frying, page 30). Line a large plate with paper towels.

Once the oil is ready, carefully lower as many wedges as will fit without crowding into the hot oil. Fry, flipping occasionally, until golden and crisp, about 3 minutes. Use a slotted spoon to transfer the panelle to the paper towels. Sprinkle with salt. Repeat to fry the remaining wedges.

Serve hot.

DEEP-FRIED RICE BALLS

arancine

MAKES 12 TO 14 ARANCINE

FOR THE FILLING

2 tablespoons olive oil

1 small onion, finely chopped

1 carrot, peeled and diced

1 celery stalk, diced

5 ounces (140 g) ground beef

5 ounces (140 g) ground pork

2 cups (480 ml) good-quality tomato sauce, homemade (page 87) or store-bought

½ cup (75 g) frozen peas

1 tablespoon estratto (sun-dried tomato paste; see Resources, page 310) or other good-quality tomato paste

½ cup (120 ml) white wine

Fine sea salt and freshly ground black pepper

FOR THE RICE

2 tablespoons olive oil

1 small onion, finely chopped

1½ cups (300 g) risotto rice, such as Carnaroli, Arborio, or Vialone Nano

2½ cups (600 ml) water

Pinch of saffron threads

3 tablespoons grated Parmigiano-Reggiano cheese

Fine sea salt and freshly ground black pepper

Found in any bar, rosticceria, or café in Sicily, arancine are considered a step above street food, a casual treat that can be equally enjoyed standing up or seated. In Palermo, the rice balls are round, while they are cone shaped in the Catania area (additionally, in Catania they are called arancini—with a final *i*—and this matter of a single letter is a point of contention between the two cities!). Ragù is the most common filling for arancine, followed closely by a version with béchamel, prosciutto, and cheese called arancina al burro. Nowadays, Sicilians make arancine often at home and fill them with all kinds of ingredients, even sweet ones filled with Nutella.

MAKE THE FILLING: In a medium saucepan, heat the olive oil over medium-high heat. Add the onion, carrot, and celery and sauté until softened, about 5 minutes. Add the meat and cook, breaking it up with a wooden spoon, until browned, 6 to 8 minutes. Add the tomato sauce and peas. In a small bowl, dissolve the estratto in the wine and add the mixture to the pan. Decrease the heat to medium-low and cook, stirring occasionally, until the sauce has thickened, about 30 minutes. Season to taste with salt and pepper and remove from the heat.

Let the filling cool completely, at least 1 hour at room temperature or in the refrigerator overnight. (Chilling the filling completely will help it to thicken, making it much easier to work with.)

Cook the rice: In a heavy-bottomed medium saucepan, heat the olive oil over medium heat, add the onion, and sauté until softened, about 8 minutes. Stir in the rice, coating the grains evenly with oil. Pour in the water and bring to a boil. As soon as the liquid boils, add the saffron. Stir well until the rice turns golden from the saffron, then cover with a lid and remove from the heat. Let sit, covered, until the rice is tender and the liquid has been fully absorbed, about 20 minutes. Stir in the Parmigiano. Taste and season with salt and pepper. Spread out the rice on a sheet pan and set aside to cool.

When the rice is cool enough to handle, prepare the coating (this is the most important step because the coating will prevent the arancine from falling apart when you deep-fry them): In a large dish with high sides, whisk together the flour, water, and eggs until

FOR THE COATING

¼ cup (30 g) all-purpose flour

2 tablespoons water

2 large eggs

2⅓ cups (250 g) plain dried
bread crumbs, plus more
for dusting

Vegetable oil, for frying

the mixture is smooth and creamy. In another dish, spread out the bread crumbs. Dust a baking sheet with bread crumbs. Place a bowl of cold water next to you.

To shape the rice balls, wet your hands in the cold water and scoop up about ¼ cup (50 g) of the rice mixture in the palm of one hand. Cup your palm and use your other hand to make a hole in the middle, pushing the rice to the same thickness all around.

Fill the hole with 1 tablespoon of filling and close your hand, enclosing the rice around the meat mixture. Add a little more rice if necessary to round out the ball. If the rice sticks to your fingers, you can wet them in the cold water. The rice ball should be no bigger than a small orange (from which the dish takes its name).

After shaping the rice ball, roll it first in the egg coating, then in the bread crumbs, making sure the ball is compact and evenly coated. Place the shaped rice ball on the crumb-dusted pan. Repeat the process to fill, shape, and roll the rest of the rice balls.

Pour about 2 inches (5 cm) of vegetable oil into a large heavy-bottomed pot and heat over medium-high heat until it is hot enough to fry in (see Deep-Frying, page 30). Line a large plate with paper towels.

Once the oil is ready, carefully place the arancine in the pan, working in batches if necessary. The rice balls may not be fully submerged in hot oil so, using a spoon, baste the top of the arancine with oil and turn them every so often to brown all sides evenly. Fry until the arancine are golden brown all over, about 3 minutes. Using a large slotted spoon, transfer them to the paper towels.

Serve hot.

NOTE: Arancine can be shaped and breaded up to 2 hours ahead of frying and refrigerated, loosely covered in plastic wrap. Any leftovers can be gently reheated in a warm oven or microwave (though they won't have the same crisp exterior as those freshly made).

RICOTTA FRITTERS

ricotta fritta

SERVES 6

1 pound (450 g) whole-milk ricotta cheese, very well drained of its liquid

Vegetable oil, for frying

3 large eggs

⅓ cup (40 g) all-purpose flour

1½ cups (185 g) plain dried bread crumbs

Fine sea salt

Plan ahead to make this appetizer—in order to hold together in the hot oil, the ricotta must be drained in a sieve for a couple of days in the fridge. The cold temperature will firm up the curds, and your patience will be rewarded with a crunchy golden bread-crumbed exterior that gives way to delicate, snow-white ricotta. Since ricotta has such a neutral flavor, you could sprinkle these with sugar and cinnamon, rather than salt, for a sweet treat.

PLACE THE DRAINED ricotta on a clean cutting board and cut into slices 1 inch (2.5 cm) thick. Cut the ricotta slices into "fingers" about 1 by 3 inches (2.5 by 7.5 cm).

Pour at least 2 inches (5 cm) of vegetable oil into a wide heavy-bottomed pot and heat over medium-high heat until it is hot enough to fry in (see Deep-Frying, page 30). Line a large plate with paper towels.

While the oil heats up, in a shallow dish, beat the eggs together with the flour. In another dish, spread out the bread crumbs. Dip each piece of ricotta in the egg mixture first and then evenly coat with the bread crumbs. Set aside.

Once the oil is ready, carefully lower a few pieces of breaded ricotta into the hot oil and fry until golden brown all over, about 1 minute. Use a slotted spoon to transfer the fried ricotta to the paper towels and season with salt. Continue with the remaining ricotta.

Serve hot.

DEEP-FRYING

THERE IS SOMETHING VERY COMFORTING ABOUT PROPERLY deep-fried food, and deep-frying has an important place in Sicilian kitchens—perhaps not every day but certainly for big, festive meals and special treats. Even though the United States and many other countries are very accustomed to eating deep-fried food, many people are scared about the act of frying itself. Lots of questions arise: What type of oil should I use? How do I know when the oil is ready? How do I know when something is done? What should I do with the leftover oil? Can I reuse it?

Contrary to popular belief, olive oil is rarely used for deep-frying, for a number of reasons: It is more expensive than many other oils, it can burn more easily, and its strong flavor might overshadow that of the food being fried. Of course, there are exceptions. In Sicily, any farmer who owns enough olive trees to produce oil for their family will save some of the less precious stock for deep-frying. In this case, "less precious" does not mean a second press (no such thing exists today in professional mills) but simply a batch that comes from a less select quality of olives. These days, Sicilians generally use a seed oil such as sunflower for deep-frying, saving the good extra-virgin olive oil for cooking at lower temperatures, which preserves its flavor and integrity.

To deep-fry successfully, an abundance of oil is key, as the ingredients must fully float in it. It is also important to have the oil at the right temperature. Sicilians rarely use a thermometer when deep-frying, knowing when the oil is ready either from experience or by testing it by dipping a piece of bread in the hot oil: If the oil around it sizzles right away, you are ready to go. If you do want to use a thermometer for the recipes in this book, fry in the range of 350° to 375°F (180° to 190°C).

Once the oil is the right temperature, gently slip in a few pieces of whatever you're cooking, taking care not to overcrowd the pan (which will cause the temperature to fall too much). Don't be scared—neither the ingredients nor the oil will splash you unless you rush as you drop in the pieces. Now is the time for patience and attention. Don't start anxiously poking the ingredients—the shock between the temperature of the ingredient and the temperature of the oil will seal the ingredient's surfaces, so the more you touch this surface, the more you risk breaking it and letting the oil penetrate. Give food the space and

time to go through the process. After a minute or so, you can start gently flipping the pieces to make sure they are frying evenly. It's good to have tongs or a slotted spoon for flipping and removing the food from the hot oil. Before you start frying, set up a large plate covered with paper towels or a sheet pan fitted with a wire rack for draining the fried food.

Sicilians tend to avoid reusing oil, unless it is for the same type of food (for instance, oil used for frying fish calls again for fish; otherwise any other food you fry in it will have a fishy taste). However, if you plan to reuse the oil, it is very important to filter the used oil in order to remove all of the little crumbs of food that gathered during frying. These bits and pieces will burn in subsequent batches, affecting the taste and causing the oil to break down more quickly. When it's time to get rid of the used oil for good, let it cool completely, then pour it into a sealable container, such as an old glass jar, and dispose of it in the trash, unless you have a local disposal spot where used cooking oil is accepted. No matter what type of oil you use, store it in a cool, dark place to keep it fresher longer.

FRIED SEAFOOD

fritto misto di pesce

SERVES 4

1½ pounds (700 g) mixed small seafood, such as shrimp, small mullets, squid, cuttlefish, and sardines

2 cups (320 g) semolina flour

Vegetable oil, for frying

Fine sea salt

Lemon wedges, for serving

Once upon a time, fritto misto was made with the unwanted catch that was unlucky enough to get tangled in the nets when fishermen were trolling for larger, more precious fish. Anything too small to sell got tossed in the fryer. Nowadays, fritto misto is a typical restaurant dish served very simply with lemon wedges. The classic components are squid, cuttlefish, shrimp, and any baby fish such as sardines, anchovies, or very small cod—but of course the idea is just to use what you can find, as long as the fish is very small and tender. For best results, fry each type of fish separately, as their cooking times may vary, and be ready to serve the dish right way.

CLEAN THE FISH and pat it dry with paper towels. Cut any large pieces into smaller ones if necessary (for instance, cut larger squid into rings). Place the semolina in a large shallow bowl.

Pour at least 2 inches (5 cm) of vegetable oil into a wide heavy-bottomed pot and heat over medium-high heat until it is hot enough to fry in (see Deep-Frying, page 30). Line a large plate with paper towels.

While the oil heats up, work with one type of fish at a time and dredge it in the flour, shaking off any excess.

Once the oil is ready, fry each type of fish separately, lowering it carefully into the oil and frying until golden all over, 1 to 2 minutes per batch. Use a slotted spoon to transfer the fish to the paper towels. Continue with the remaining fish.

Transfer the fried fish to a serving platter, sprinkle with salt, and serve at once, with lemon wedges on the side.

MUSSEL GRATIN

gratin di cozze

SERVES 6

2 pounds (900 g) mussels

2 large tomatoes, chopped

1 garlic clove, finely chopped

2 tablespoons olive oil, plus more for drizzling

1¼ cups (155 g) plain dried bread crumbs

2 tablespoons finely chopped fresh flat-leaf parsley

Finely grated zest of 1 lemon

1 tablespoon dried oregano, preferably wild (see Resources, page 310)

Fine sea salt and freshly ground black pepper

Served in their shells, these juicy mussels topped with a brightly flavored bread crumb topping can be eaten out of hand as a casual appetizer or with a fork as a plated dish. The same bread crumb mixture could be used to top clams or oysters.

WASH THE MUSSELS carefully under cold water, scrubbing off any grit and pulling away the beards. Put the mussels in a large dry pan (no liquid added) and cook them uncovered over medium-high heat, stirring occasionally, just until they open, 3 to 5 minutes. Remove from the heat. Set a large sieve over a bowl and drain the mussels, reserving the liquid that collects in the bowl. (Discard any that don't open.) When the mussels are cool enough to handle, pull off the top shells, leaving the mussels attached to the bottom shells (discard the empty shells). Arrange the shells with the mussels attached on a large baking sheet. Set aside.

In a medium skillet, combine the tomatoes, garlic, and 1 tablespoon of the olive oil and cook over medium heat, stirring occasionally, until reduced to a light sauce, about 10 minutes. Scrape the sauce into a bowl and return the skillet to the stove.

Heat the remaining 1 tablespoon olive oil over medium heat. Add the bread crumbs and cook, stirring, until they are beginning to toast, about 2 minutes. Add the parsley, lemon zest, and oregano. Season with salt and pepper. Continue to cook, stirring constantly, until the bread crumbs are toasted and golden brown, about 3 minutes. Remove from the heat and stir in 1 cup (240 ml) of the tomato mixture and about 2 tablespoons of the reserved mussel cooking liquid (you may have some tomato sauce left over). The mixture should hold together and be somewhat sticky.

Preheat the oven to 350°F (180°C).

Fill the shells, adding just enough of the bread crumb mixture to fully cover each mussel, and set them back on the baking sheet. Drizzle some olive oil over the shells and bake for 10 minutes. Remove from the oven and sprinkle some of the reserved mussel liquid over the mussels. Return to the oven and broil until the bread crumbs are well toasted, 3 to 5 minutes.

Remove from the oven and serve at once.

NOTE: The mussels can be cooked and topped with the bread crumb mixture up to 6 hours in advance. Refrigerate, covered in plastic wrap, until you are ready to bake them.

OCTOPUS SALAD

insalata di polipo

-photo page 18-

SERVES 6 TO 8

Fine sea salt

**1 whole octopus
(2 pounds/900 g), cleaned**

¼ cup (60 ml) olive oil

**2 tablespoons fresh
lemon juice**

**2 tablespoons finely chopped
fresh flat-leaf parsley**

Sicily's seafood restaurants often greet you with displays of boiled whole octopuses propped up on large colorful platters—a dramatic sight! Unlike most people, Sicilians prefer their octopus more chewy than tender. In order to get the curly tentacles, you must hold the octopus by the head and plunge it into boiling water three times before leaving it to simmer gently. The dressing for this salad is exceedingly simple—lemon, parsley, and olive oil—and so the secret to success here lies in the freshness of the octopus and cooking it properly.

BRING A LARGE pot of salted water to a boil. Holding the octopus by its head, plunge it into the boiling water three times, then leave it in the water and simmer until tender, 30 to 40 minutes. Remove from the pot and let cool.

In a small bowl, stir together the olive oil, lemon juice, and parsley. Chop the octopus into bite-size pieces and place in a shallow bowl. Pour the dressing over it and toss gently to combine. Season to taste with salt. Serve the octopus salad cold or at room temperature.

NOTE: The octopus salad can be made up to 6 hours ahead and refrigerated until serving time.

OLIVE OIL

DRIVING ALMOST ANYWHERE IN SICILY, FROM THE COAST TO
the mountains, you will see olive groves. The trees may be
planted in tidy rows on large smooth hills, in small patches
dotting vast wheat fields, or at the edges of a vineyard, their
gray-green leaves waving in the breeze. An olive tree grows
very slowly, not just in height but also in girth, as its trunk widens
with bumps and knobs and develops mysterious cavities
and twists. A healthy olive tree may grow and bear fruit for
thousands of years, a living monument to Mother Nature. An
Italian saying beautifully illustrates that longevity: "I plant the
vineyard, my father plants the mulberry, and my grandfather
plants the olive tree."

The olive tree, ubiquitous throughout the Mediterranean
landscape and culture, arrived in Sicily with the Greeks, who
revered it, considering the tree a symbol of knowledge and vital
energy. At the time, olive oil was mainly used as an ointment or
balm, not for culinary purposes. The Romans were the ones who
figured out how to make really good olive oil—by harvesting the
olives directly from the tree and pressing them right away—as
well as every possible way to make use of the fruit and its oil
for cooking. But with the fall of the Roman Empire, Sicily's oil
production declined sharply. A new culture had come in from
northern Europe that was more keen on lard and butter (since
their climate could not support olive crops), and therefore many
Italian farmers abandoned their olive oil production and the
good practices set up by the Romans were lost. Many Sicilian
farmers would pick overripe olives in order to get more fat
content, then store them improperly before pressing them in large
woven baskets made out of hemp, called fiscoli. The results were
of dubious value, since the olives were often rancid by the time
they made it to press, and the baskets were impossible to clean.

Fortunately, the knowledge, process, and technology
of olive oil production have hugely improved in the last fifty
years. In fall, when the olives have reached the right degree of
ripeness—half green and half purple—the trees are surrounded
by nets, and groups of men use sticks or mechanical combs to
knock down the olives, which are then collected in large crates
and brought straight to the press. Most Sicilian olive oil today is
excellent and extremely diverse, thanks to its many cultivars and

terroir. Sicilian olive growers experiment with a wide array of cultivars, including Biancolilla, Cerasuola, Nocellara del Belice, Tonda Iblea, Moresca, Ogliarola Messinese, Nocellara Etnea, Giarraffa, and Santagatese. There is new awareness about how important each stage of ripeness is and how that, along with proper processing, can determine quality, pungency, and flavor compounds. The dream of any good olive oil producer today is to offer a number of choices and flavors to pair with different foods, as we are accustomed to doing with wine.

That said, the olive oil business has a long history of fraud and corruption, and it can be hard for consumers to know what to trust. The shelf life of good olive oil is usually one and a half years from the date of harvest, but very few producers indicate that date. You may find yourself with olive oil that was harvested at a certain time but bottled years later or that has been blended with inferior oils. Price can be a good indicator of quality. But the best way to learn how to identify good olive oil is just to taste, taste, taste. Regularly seeking out olive oil from reliable producers will help the consumer and cook build an invaluable internal compass.

CITRUS-MARINATED SARDINES

sarde marinate

SERVES 4

½ pound (225 g) very fresh small sardines or anchovies, heads removed, cleaned and boned (see Cleaning Fresh Sardines and Anchovies, page 134)

Juice of 2 lemons

Juice of 1 orange

1 small loaf good-quality semolina bread, thinly sliced

¼ cup (60 ml) olive oil

1 garlic clove, halved

1 tablespoon dried oregano, preferably wild (see Resources, page 310)

Fine sea salt and freshly ground black pepper

Crudo di pesce, a relatively new staple on menus in Sicily's coastal cities, is usually a combination of swordfish, tuna, and grouper served thinly sliced, carpaccio-style. Another common antipasto is whole, raw sardines marinated in vinegar and seasoned with olive oil. This version calls instead for fresh lemon and orange juices, which give a sweeter, mellower flavor. Served on semolina toasts and drizzled with oregano-flecked olive oil, these summery sardines are the perfect accompaniment to some chilled amaro or other aperitivo.

PLACE THE CLEANED sardines in a small bowl and pour the lemon and orange juices over them. Marinate for 20 to 30 minutes.

Meanwhile, preheat the broiler. Arrange the bread on a baking sheet and broil until lightly toasted, about 3 minutes, flipping halfway through.

In a small bowl, combine the olive oil, garlic, oregano, and salt to taste. Drain the sardines, and one at a time dip in the olive oil mixture and arrange on a slice of toasted bread. Sprinkle with salt and pepper and serve at once.

SAUTÉED BLACK OLIVES

olive nere saltate

MAKES ABOUT 2 CUPS
(350 G)

2 cups (350 g) black olives

Finely grated zest of 1 orange

1 small dried hot chile, chopped, or a pinch of crushed red pepper flakes

3 tablespoons olive oil

½ teaspoon dark brown sugar

½ teaspoon dried oregano, preferably wild (see Resources, page 310)

Warming olives helps their flavors and those of the aromatics really bloom. Serve these with a selection of antipasti, such as Chickpea Fritters (page 22) and Octopus Salad (page 37).

IN A MEDIUM skillet, combine the olives, orange zest, chile, olive oil, brown sugar, and oregano and cook gently over medium heat, stirring occasionally, until the sugar is dissolved. Serve warm.

NOTE: Leftover olives can be refrigerated for up to 1 week. Reheat gently before serving.

OLIVES

AN OLIVE'S COLOR IS DETERMINED BY WHEN IT IS HARVESTED.
All olives are green as they grow on the tree, becoming deep
purple and finally black as they ripen. Accordingly, green olives
are generally quite firm, while black olives, being riper, are softer
and juicier. More than thirty different olive cultivars are grown
in Sicily; some are used for pressing into olive oil, and some are
distinguished as olive da tavola (table olives). The most common
green olives used for pickling are Nocellara and Zaituna, from
western Sicily and the area around Siracusa in the southeast.
As for black olives, Giarraffa and Piricuddara generally grow
around Agrigento and in central Sicily. Raw olives are unbearably
bitter, so they must be cured, either in salt or in a brine.

Green olives are typically cured in a brine made of salt and
water, which may be seasoned with garlic, bay leaves, and
possibly some wild fennel. Black olives are salted and set out to
dry in the sun or in the oven. Olives have long been a staple in
the Sicilian peasant diet—cured olives and a hunk of bread were
easy to carry around the fields and might have served as the sole
midday meal. Today, olives are used in salads, to cook with, for
seasoning focaccia, or served just as a nibble before the meal.

If you get your hands on fresh olives and would like to try
curing them yourself, here are the basics: For green olives, make
a brine of ⅓ cup (100 g) fine sea salt for every 1 quart (1 L) water,
making enough to completely cover the amount of olives you
have. Place the fresh green olives in a large bucket and cover
with the brine, adding a few cloves of garlic, bay leaves, and
some wild fennel fronds, if possible. Let sit, covered, in a cool,
dark place, until the olives are cured and taste pleasantly bitter,
about 3 months.

To cure black olives, stir together 1 cup (300 g) fine sea salt
for every 4½ pounds (2 kg) fresh black olives in a large bowl and
let sit for 5 days, stirring the olives once a day. The olives will
release their moisture. Taste the olives after 5 days. If they are to
your liking, drain off the liquid that has collected and store the
olives in jars or vacuum-sealed bags. They may also be frozen.

Once you've cured your olives (or picked up some from your
favorite shop), see page 41 and page 43 for two delicious ways
to serve them.

GREEN OLIVE SALAD

insalata di olive verdi

MAKES ABOUT 2¼ CUPS
(ABOUT 500 G)

**2 cups (350 g) cured
green olives**

½ small red onion, sliced

1 small carrot, chopped

**1 celery stalk with some
tender leaves, chopped**

**1 tablespoon dried oregano,
preferably wild (see
Resources, page 310)**

3 tablespoons olive oil

**2 teaspoons red or white
wine vinegar**

These olives make a tasty nibble before dinner, but they
also taste great alongside a main course like Mackerel Confit
(page 138) or Sicilian Meatloaf (page 184).

PLACE THE OLIVES in a colander and rinse under running water to
remove excess salt. Shake dry. Transfer the olives to a medium bowl
and add the onion, carrot, celery, and oregano. Stir in the olive oil
and vinegar. Serve at room temperature.

NOTE: Leftover olive salad can be refrigerated for up to 1 week.

AMARO

BITTERNESS IS CERTAINLY AN ACQUIRED TASTE BUT ONE THAT is embedded in Sicily's regional culture, as evidenced by the love and appreciation for foods such as wild greens and chicories, fava beans, artichokes, and bitter almonds. Sicilians also love bitter drinks—dark cups of espresso, Campari and Aperol spritzes, and all sorts of other liqueurs flavored with herbs, known collectively as amari. Amaro Averna was created in Caltanissetta at the end of the nineteenth century when a monk gifted the recipe for the dark concoction to a local man, Salvatore Averna, in gratitude for his generous charity work. Averna, now owned by Campari, is enjoyed worldwide as a postprandial digestive. Indeed, many amari were traditionally made in Italy by monks, and now those recipes have been passed on. In Sicily, new generations of farmers are experimenting with all sorts of bitter flavors and discovering new herbs to macerate in alcohol and turn into amari. These bright, bittersweet drinks make a good foil for antipasti, balancing out the often rich notes of fried or tangy bites.

ARTICHOKES PRESERVED IN OIL

carciofi sott'olio

MAKES ENOUGH TO FILL FOUR
8-OUNCE (240 ML) JARS

2 lemons, halved

12 to 15 small artichokes

1 quart (1 L) distilled
white vinegar

2 cups (500 ml) water

1 teaspoon black peppercorns

4 bay leaves

3 garlic cloves

2 tablespoons fine sea salt

12 to 16 whole cloves

2 cups (500 ml) neutral-
flavored oil, such as
grapeseed

2 cups (500 ml) olive oil

Preserved artichokes are often made with the last crop of the season, sometime in April. The artichokes are harvested when they are still small and very tender. (This recipe won't work with large artichokes.) The best variety for this preparation is the spinoso from Menfi, a coastal town near Trapani. This small, oval-shaped artichoke with violet-tinged leaves grows from November to late April. Its thorny leaves are somewhat difficult to handle, but getting to its heart—crisp, juicy, and delicately flavored—is well worth the work. Serve these on a charcuterie board or on their own with good bread.

SQUEEZE THE JUICE from the lemons into a large bowl of cool water and drop in the squeezed halves. Break off and discard all the tough outer leaves of each artichoke. Working with one artichoke at a time, halve it lengthwise through the stem. Remove and discard any fluffy choke in the middle using the tip of a sharp knife. Cut the artichoke again lengthwise into 2 or 3 wedges (depending on its size) and place them in the prepared lemon bath.

To prepare the jars, bring a large pot of water to a boil. Wash four 8-ounce (240 ml) canning jars and screw-top lids (the kind with a metal ring and a flat, rubber-edged top) with hot, soapy water. Sterilize the jars and lids in the boiling water for at least 10 minutes. Remove the jars using jar lifters or tongs, drain well, and set aside to dry on a clean surface.

In a large pot, bring the vinegar and water to a boil. Add the peppercorns, bay leaves, garlic cloves, and salt. Line a sheet pan with a clean kitchen towel and have nearby.

Drain the artichokes (discard the spent lemon halves). Add the artichokes to the boiling brine and cook until slightly softened but still a little crunchy, 2 to 3 minutes. Use a slotted spoon to transfer the artichokes to the prepared sheet pan. Pat dry.

Put 3 or 4 whole cloves in each sterilized jar. Fill the jars with the artichokes, pressing lightly. In a spouted measuring cup, combine the oils and pour into the jars to cover the artichokes, leaving ½ inch (1 cm) of space at the top of each jar. Run a clean knife down the sides of each jar to release any air bubbles. Make sure all artichokes are covered with oil before screwing on the lids. They'll be ready to enjoy in a week or two.

NOTE: Jarred artichokes can be stored in a cool, dark place for up to 1 year.

recipe continues

ZUCCHINI PRESERVED IN OIL

zucchine sott'olio

Make these preserves when zucchini are overrunning your garden; they are delicious with grilled meat or on bruschetta.

USING A MANDOLINE, slice 4½ pounds (2 kg) medium zucchini lengthwise into very thin ribbons, avoiding the seedy core (discard the core). Arrange the ribbons in a single layer on wire racks and let them dry in the hot sun until they're mostly dehydrated but still pliable. Depending on the weather, this could take a couple of hours or a full day. (Alternatively, dry them in a food dehydrator.) Sterilize the jars and lids as directed. In a large pot, bring 1 quart (1 L) distilled white vinegar, 2 cups (500 ml) water, and 2 tablespoons fine sea salt to a boil. Add the zucchini and boil until tender, 2 to 3 minutes. Drain well and blot dry with a clean kitchen towel. In a bowl, season the zucchini with a drizzle of olive oil, a few pinches of dried oregano, and 1 minced garlic clove. Pack the zucchini mixture into the prepared jars and proceed with the recipe as directed, filling the jars with an equal amount of neutral seed oil and olive oil. They'll be ready to enjoy in a week or two. Jarred zucchini can be stored in a cool, dark place for up to 1 year.

MUSHROOMS PRESERVED IN OIL

funghi sott'olio

Oyster mushrooms work perfectly for these preserves.

CLEAN 2 POUNDS (900 g) mushrooms by brushing away any dirt with a dry paper towel (don't use water). Cut away any hard stems and cut the mushrooms into thick strips. Prepare a large pot with 2 cups (500 ml) distilled white vinegar and 2 cups (500 ml) water. Add 1 tablespoon coriander seeds, 2 tablespoons black peppercorns, and 4 or 5 bay leaves. Bring to a boil, then add the mushrooms. Once the mixture returns to a boil, remove from the heat. Use a slotted spoon to transfer the mushrooms to a sheet pan lined with a clean kitchen towel. Blot the mushrooms with a kitchen towel and let sit until dry, 1 to 3 hours. Transfer the mushrooms to jars that have been sterilized as directed and fill the jars with an equal amount of neutral seed oil and olive oil. They'll be ready to enjoy in a week or two. Jarred mushrooms can be stored in a cool, dark place for up to 1 year.

PRESERVING FOOD

THERE ARE MANY DIFFERENT WAYS TO PRESERVE FOOD, WITH each part of the world taking its cues from its own resources and climate. For instance, many northern European countries, with their abundant forests and cool weather, rely on smoking. Most of Sicily's woodlands were chopped down centuries ago in order to build ships for the Roman army, so smoking isn't an option here. When it comes to preserving, the island turns to what it does have in abundance: salt and sun. Salt is harvested from the surrounding sea as well as mines in the Madonie Mountains, which are still some of the largest in Europe (see Mountains, page 172). It is not difficult to dehydrate vegetables and fruits in a place where temperatures can rise above 100°F (40°C) in summer. Fungi and bacteria thrive in the presence of water and oxygen, so drying food is a good way to "sanitize" it. Sun, salt, brine, vinegar, and olive oil . . . these are the traditional ways that Sicilians preserve and keep their bounty.

August is the peak of the summer heat, so this is when farmers and cooks start laying out the fruits of their gardens, whatever dries easily under the hot sun, knowing that they must take advantage of this moment in order to be able to enjoy these ingredients year-round. Traveling around the island, one will often bump into large tables covered with halved tomatoes, sliced zucchini hanging like ribbons, and garlands of plump figs, their flavors concentrating as their moisture evaporates under the intense summer sun.

Come fall, attention turns to curing both black and green olives, brining mushrooms, and making the beloved quince paste known as cotognata. Winter is the time for marmalades and candied peel made from all of the island's beautiful citrus. April, May, and June are the months for making jam from sour cherries, peaches, plums, and apricots and canning artichokes and tuna.

Over the years, the culture of preserves has evolved; it is no longer tied to famine and necessity but today is simply a way to transform an ingredient into something delightful, different, and delicious. Jarred artichokes, eggplants, olives, caper leaves, cucunci (caper berries), and zucchini, among other treats, are now considered a delicacy and are served in households and restaurants for the sole pleasure of having those foods at the table when they are out of season.

SOUPS

minestre

FAVA BEAN SOUP WITH POACHED EGGS 57
macco di fave con uova in camicia

CHICKPEA SOUP WITH TUMA CHEESE 62
minestra di ceci

LENTIL SOUP 65
minestra di lenticchie

ESCAROLE SOUP 66
minestra di scarola

TENERUMI SOUP 7O
minestra di tenerumi e cucuzze

FISH SOUP WITH STEAMED COUSCOUS 72
zuppa di pesce con cùscus

n Sicily, the word *minestra* refers to brothy soups made of vegetables and legumes that were meant to sustain laborers and farmers after a long day's work. Though they could serve, like pasta, as a primo piatto, these rustic soups, thickened with pasta, rice, potato, or bread, often comprised the main evening meal, all on their own. Indeed, minestra has nothing in common with the sort of consommé that would signal the start of any banquet in an aristocratic household.

Due to necessity and circumstance, these soups were most often vegetarian, with lentils, chickpeas, or fava beans providing the necessary protein. While minestra is still a staple dish for Sicilians today, it must be noted that some (and by "some," we mean mostly men) still consider it a sort of second-class food compared to meat. *U megghiu bruodo è la carne* ("The best broth is meat") is a saying that explains how a region that has dealt with starvation for centuries might crave a joint of lamb or a pork roast more than a vegetarian soup.

However, for young children, the ill, the infirm, and especially those in mourning, minestra was and still is a comfort food of the first order. After a death in the family, there used to be a custom called *u counsulo* ("the consolation"), a period when the household could not use the kitchen stove and had to rely on their neighbors to cook for them. In such cases, soup was almost considered medicine, its warm comfort full of healing properties sliding gently from throat to stomach. In everyday life, minestra may be considered an insignificant food, but in special moments of human life—birth, sickness, death—as well as in certain ritual occasions, it becomes essential!

During many Sicilian feast days, soups made of legumes or grains act as a sort of "seed" of grace and faith for those who share it. The celebration of Saint Joseph, on March 19, is one such occasion. In the past, to thank the saint for protecting their families, the town mothers would each build an altar, in many cases a long table set up in the largest room of the house, and fill it with all sorts of foods. They would then open their doors to the poorest of the town and welcome them in to eat. In rural Sicily, which always had the strongest tradition of celebrating Saint Joseph, this ritual was a gentle way to keep the community together and to support those living in poverty. In more recent times, since the late twentieth century, the altar has transformed into one communal table and the ritual into a collective feast. Anyone can contribute, and everyone is welcome.

Most Sicilian soups start by sautéing some diced onion, perhaps with a clove of garlic, in plenty of olive oil. A teaspoon of tomato paste diluted with wine or water may be stirred in, or a few salted anchovies added, to nudge up the savoriness. Gentleness is key—the flavors of the onion, garlic, and tomato should marry so that you end up with a rich, flavorful base to which you simply add water (Sicilians rarely use stock) and whatever vegetables or legumes are called for. Such a preparation allows the ingredients to sing rather than become muffled behind a meaty broth.

FAVA BEAN SOUP WITH POACHED EGGS

macco di fave con uova in camicia

SERVES 6

1 red onion, finely chopped

½ cup (120 ml) olive oil, plus more for drizzling

1¾ pounds (800 g) shelled, blanched, and peeled fava beans (see Notes)

7 ounces (200 g) wild fennel (optional; see Wild Fennel, page 101), chopped

1 bay leaf

Fine sea salt

1 quart (1 L) hot water, plus more as needed

6 large eggs

Freshly ground black pepper

Macco is an ancient fava bean soup that is both earthy and bright, tasting of all that is fresh and green. Designed to herald the beginning of spring and the hopes for an abundant harvest, macco is traditionally served for the Feast of Saint Joseph on March 19, which generally falls during Lent, when Catholics are supposed to fast. The tricky part is knowing how many fresh fava bean pods to buy in order to get the correct amount of shelled and peeled beans for making this soup. Though each pod yields a slightly different amount, know that about 6 pounds (2.75 kg) fresh fava bean pods should give you enough beans for this recipe. Of course, you can always cut to the chase and buy frozen shelled favas ready to go. Indeed, many Sicilian households generally spend a day or two blanching, peeling, and freezing fava beans in spring so they can make this soup all year round. If you aren't able to find wild fennel, just leave it out—the soup will still be delicious.

IN A LARGE pot, cook the onion in the olive oil over medium heat until very light golden, 2 to 3 minutes. Add the peeled fava beans and stir to coat them in oil. Mix in the wild fennel (if using), bay leaf, and a big pinch of salt. Pour in the hot water and bring to a boil, then reduce the heat and simmer gently, partially covered, until the fava beans break down to a chunky puree, 20 to 25 minutes.

Use an immersion blender to puree the soup. (Alternatively, carefully transfer the soup to a countertop blender and puree until smooth.) If the soup is thicker than you'd like, thin it with a little hot water. Season with more salt to taste. Keep warm, covered and stirring occasionally, over very low heat.

To poach the eggs, bring a small saucepan of water to a simmer. Line a plate with paper towels. Crack an egg into a small cup. Use a spoon to gently swirl the water in the saucepan to create a little whirlpool. Lower the cup with the egg into the center of the whirlpool, then swiftly lift out the cup, leaving the egg behind. Give the water another stir to encourage the egg white to stay close to its yolk. Simmer until the white is set but the yolk is still runny, 2 to 3 minutes. Use a slotted spoon to transfer the egg to the prepared plate. Repeat with the remaining eggs.

Serve each bowl of soup topped with a poached egg, a drizzle of olive oil, and a sprinkle of black pepper.

recipe continues

NOTES

- If you buy fresh favas in their pods, they will need to be shelled and peeled. To make it easier to peel them, they should first be lightly blanched. Bring a pot of water to a boil. While the water heats, remove the fava beans from their pods. Add the fava beans to the boiling water and cook until they turn bright green and look loose in their skins, about 2 minutes. Drain. When the favas are cool enough to handle, peel and discard the skins. The peeled beans are now ready to be made into macco, or you can freeze them for a later use.

- The soup can be made up to 3 days ahead, cooled completely, and refrigerated. It will thicken as it sits. Reheat gently over medium-low heat, adding water as needed to thin it.

LEGUMES

LEGUMES, SUCH AS CHICKPEAS, LENTILS, AND FAVA BEANS, have historically been the main source of protein for Sicilians, who often serve fresh or dried beans with carbohydrate-rich pasta. Such combinations are not only delicious but also nutritionally sound: On their own, legumes and pasta do not have all the essential amino acids necessary to become a complete protein, but bringing them together in one dish does. (Rinsing the dried beans several times before soaking them, in the case of chickpeas, or cooking them, as for lentils, will also help make them easier to digest.) Pasta with lentils, pasta with chickpeas, pasta with fava beans . . . these dishes have helped Sicilians, who so often sat down to a meatless table, survive for millennia.

Legumes, especially favas, have also been essential to Sicilian farmers. Before the existence of chemical fertilizers, farmers kept their soil healthy through thoughtful crop rotation, intercropping, and the use of manure. Legumes are a rotation crop that returns nitrogen, depleted by growing wheat, to the soil thanks to a symbiotic relationship between the roots and bacteria called rhizobia, which transform the oxygen in the air into nitrogen and fix it in the soil. Farmers plant a variety of favas called favino for just this purpose: When the plants have flowered in spring but before they have produced beans, the area is tilled so that the root system and rhizobia "feed" the soil while the leafy greens act as a mulch.

OPPOSITE: *Rows of lentil plants growing in central Sicily.*

FOLLOWING PAGE: *Dried beans, nuts, and spices are often sold together at local markets.*

CHICKPEA SOUP WITH TUMA CHEESE

minestra di ceci

SERVES 6 TO 8

1¾ cups (350 g) dried
chickpeas

1 medium yellow onion,
finely chopped

¼ cup (60 ml) olive oil

1 tomato, peeled and diced,
or 1 tablespoon estratto
(sun-dried tomato paste; see
Resources, page 310) or other
good-quality tomato paste

½ cup (100 g) chopped wild
fennel or a combination of
equal parts fresh dill and
parsley (optional)

1 garlic clove, finely chopped

2 bay leaves

3 quarts (3 L) water

Fine sea salt and freshly
ground black pepper

9 ounces (250 g) ditalini
pasta

6 ounces (170 g) tuma cheese
or provola, cut into small
dice

Dried oregano, preferably
wild (see Resources,
page 310), for serving

In Sicily, farmers grow mainly two types of chickpeas: black, which are difficult to soften fully and therefore digest, and the more familiar buff-colored ones. Among the latter, the most delicious are a variety called Pascià, which are grown in the area around Palermo. Nicely plump, they produce a rich, creamy texture ideal for this hearty soup. You can still find a few shops and street vendors in Palermo that sell all kinds of dried legumes, as well as seeds and nuts, piled high in big bags like you see in the souks of Marrakesh and Casablanca.

THE NIGHT BEFORE you plan to make the soup, place the chickpeas in a bowl and cover with plenty of water. Set aside to soak overnight.

The next day, in a large pot, cook the onion in the olive oil over medium heat, stirring occasionally, until the onion is soft, 8 to 10 minutes. Add the tomato, wild fennel (if using), garlic, and bay leaves. Drain the soaked chickpeas and add them to the pot. Stir to coat everything in oil. Pour in the 3 quarts (3 L) water and bring to a boil. Reduce the heat so that the soup simmers gently, cover the pot, and cook until the chickpeas are tender, 2 to 3 hours. While the soup simmers, periodically skim off any foam that collects on the surface and discard.

When the chickpeas are fully tender, season to taste with salt and pepper. Add the pasta to the soup and cook until al dente, about 8 minutes.

To serve, ladle the hot soup into bowls and top with a spoonful of the diced cheese and a pinch of dried oregano.

NOTE: The soup, up to the pasta step, can be made up to 3 days ahead, cooled completely, and refrigerated. Reheat gently, adding more water as needed to thin it, then add the pasta and continue as directed.

LENTIL SOUP

minestra di lenticchie

SERVES 4 TO 6

2 garlic cloves, smashed and peeled

¼ cup (60 ml) olive oil, plus more for drizzling

1 medium onion, chopped

2 small carrots, chopped

1 tomato, peeled and chopped, or 1 tablespoon estratto (sun-dried tomato paste; see Resources, page 310) or other good-quality tomato paste

2 bay leaves

Fine sea salt and freshly ground black pepper

2 cups (400 g) lentils

1 small potato, peeled and coarsely chopped

2½ quarts (2.5 L) water

Chopped fresh flat-leaf parsley, for serving

The small town of Villalba in central Sicily is especially famous for its lentils, which are plump and green and hold their shape while cooking. Ustica, a small island about 40 miles (65 km) off the coast of Palermo, is prized for another variety that is more brown than green and quite small. Both work very well in this rustic soup. A bit of potato is added to help thicken it, but a handful of dried pasta or rice could be used instead.

IN A MEDIUM pot, cook the garlic in the olive oil over medium heat, stirring occasionally, until fragrant and golden, 2 to 3 minutes. Add the onion and carrots and stir to coat with the oil. Cook, stirring occasionally, until the vegetables are beginning to soften, about 5 minutes. Add the tomato and bay leaves and cook, stirring, for 2 minutes. Season with ½ teaspoon salt and ½ teaspoon pepper. Add the lentils, potato, and water and bring to a boil. Reduce the heat to a simmer, partially cover, and cook gently until the lentils are tender and the soup has thickened, 1½ to 2 hours. Taste and adjust the seasonings.

Serve the soup drizzled with olive oil and sprinkled with chopped parsley.

NOTE: The soup can be made up to 3 days ahead, cooled completely, and refrigerated. It will thicken as it sits. Reheat gently over medium-low heat, adding more water as needed to thin it.

ESCAROLE SOUP

minestra di scarola

SERVES 4

1¾ pounds (790 g) escarole

1 medium red onion, chopped

⅓ cup (80 ml) extra-virgin olive oil

6 cups (1.5 L) water

Fine sea salt

3½ ounces (100 g) pasta (either small pasta like ditalini or thin spaghetti that has been broken into short pieces)

2 ounces (57 g) provola or tuma cheese, cut into small cubes

Finely grated Parmigiano-Reggiano cheese, for serving

Escarole is rarely used as a salad green or sautéed as a side dish in Sicily but is more commonly found as an ingredient in soup or as a filling or topping for bread or pizza, like the Focaccia from Messina with Escarole and Tomatoes (page 250), a specialty of that northeastern city. Either plain or curly escarole works here. This is the kind of soup—mild and nourishing—that tastes just right after coming home from a long trip, or when you feel a little under the weather.

CHOP THE ESCAROLE leaves into 2-inch (5 cm) pieces, rinse well, and set aside in a colander to drain.

In a large pot, cook the onion in the olive oil over medium heat, stirring occasionally, until soft, 8 to 10 minutes. Add the escarole and cook for another minute, stirring to coat the leaves in oil. Add the water and 1 teaspoon salt and bring to a boil. Reduce the heat, cover, and simmer gently until the greens are tender, about 20 minutes.

Add the pasta to the soup and cook until al dente, 6 to 8 minutes. Taste the broth and season with salt if needed.

Ladle the hot soup into four serving bowls. Top with the provola and serve the Parmigiano on the side.

NOTE: The soup, up to the pasta step, can be made up to 3 days ahead, cooled completely, and refrigerated. Reheat gently before adding the pasta and continuing as directed.

SALT

ARTISANAL SEA SALT HAS BECOME VERY FASHIONABLE IN THE
last few decades, but before then, few people cared if the salt
they used while cooking was collected from the sea or mined
from a cave. Sicily produces both types of salt. Some of the
largest salt mines in Europe are found near the beautiful town of
Petralia, in the foothills of the Madonie Mountains. The mines go
down some eight stories below ground, connected by 44 miles
(70 km) of wide tunnels. Every day, huge trucks transport loads
of salt, some of it to be sold in supermarkets and some to be
shipped to the north of Italy to salt icy roads in winter.

Practically due west from Petralia, the coastal area between
Selinunte, Marsala, and Trapani is a very different world. The
land is mostly flat, with the exception of Monte Erice, which rises
abruptly to a height of 2,760 feet (840 m), and the area has been
extremely prosperous and abundant ever since the Phoenicians
first settled here around 800 BCE. These great explorers and
sailors established their first colonies in Palermo and on the island
of Saint Pantaleo (today called Mozia) between Trapani and
Marsala. There they created salt flats and began trading the
so-called "white gold" with other Mediterranean countries.

The trade is thriving today, and it is a treat to visit the shallow
ponds of water that change from blue to pink as the water
evaporates, leaving the solid mineral behind. Many of the salt
flats are still guarded by stone windmills, which once helped
move the water from pond to pond and powered the millstones
that ground the salt, as well as large pyramids of drying salt
protected by clay tiles. Only a few producers still harvest salt in
this artisanal way; the majority of production is now mechanized
(see Resources, page 310, for where to buy Sicilian salt).
Nevertheless, the pink ponds and windmills are the exceptionally
beautiful pillars of this unique landscape.

TENERUMI SOUP

minestra di tenerumi e cucuzze

SERVES 6 TO 8

1 red onion, finely chopped

2 garlic cloves, chopped

½ cup (120 ml) olive oil

2 tomatoes, chopped, or one 14.5-ounce (411 g) can diced tomatoes

Fine sea salt and freshly ground black pepper

2 pounds (900 g) small cucuzza squash or medium zucchini, peeled and chopped

8 ounces (225 g) tenerumi or other tender squash greens, chopped into 1-inch (2.5 cm) pieces

1 small bunch of celery leaves, chopped

1 potato, peeled and chopped

4 cups (1 L) lukewarm water

Cucuzza lunga is a type of pale green summer squash that can reach such great lengths—up to 5 or 6 feet (1.5 to 2 m)!—that it must hang from pergolas in order to grow properly. This classic Sicilian soup uses not just the squash but also its tender leaves, or tenerumi. The result is both soothing and refreshing and is commonly served while squash is in season, from July until September. This version calls for potato to provide a little starchiness, but it can be omitted in favor of some broken-up spaghetti or capellini cooked al dente in the soup itself just before serving.

IN A LARGE pot, cook the onion and garlic in the olive oil over medium-high heat, stirring, until the onion and garlic are golden, about 5 minutes. Add the tomatoes and cook, stirring, for 2 to 3 minutes. Season lightly with salt and pepper. Stir in the squash, squash greens, celery leaves, and potato and cook for another 2 minutes. Pour in the water and bring to a boil. Reduce the heat to a gentle simmer, cover, and cook until the vegetables are tender, 20 to 25 minutes.

Taste and season with a little more salt and pepper if you like. Serve hot.

NOTES

- If you can't find tenerumi or squash greens, other tender greens, such as chard leaves or spinach, can be substituted.
- The soup can be made up to 3 days ahead, cooled completely, and refrigerated.

FISH SOUP WITH STEAMED COUSCOUS

zuppa di pesce con cùscus

SERVES 8

FOR THE FISH AND BROTH

About 4½ pounds (2 kg) whole fish, such as mullet, cod, red snapper, and/or grouper

2 tablespoons olive oil

⅓ cup (80 ml) white wine

3 celery stalks, including their leaves

2 carrots, peeled

2 medium onions, peeled and halved

3 garlic cloves, peeled

1 tablespoon estratto (sun-dried tomato paste; see Resources, page 310) or other good-quality tomato paste

1 tablespoon black peppercorns

1 tablespoon juniper berries

8 cardamom pods

2 cinnamon sticks

1 teaspoon fine sea salt

4 quarts (4 L) water

FOR THE COUSCOUS

2¾ cups (500 g) fine traditional couscous (not instant; see page 77)

½ cup (120 ml) water

1 small onion, finely chopped

4 garlic cloves, finely chopped

½ cup (20 g) finely chopped fresh flat-leaf parsley, plus more for garnish

The western cities of Trapani and Marsala are the main areas of Sicily where couscous dishes have traditionally been made. And to differentiate Sicilian couscous from the Moroccan and Tunisian versions, which are almost always made with meat, Sicilians prepare theirs mainly with fish, following the tradition of fishermen who would use their unsold fish—the leftovers with little commercial value—to make soup and season the couscous. *Non è buono manco per fare cùscus* ("He is no good, not even to make couscous") is a saying still used to refer to someone who is utterly useless.

Today, many cooks still use lesser-quality fish to make the stock and then one prized fish to fillet and poach gently in the soup before serving with the couscous (but make sure you add that fish's carcass to the stockpot, too!). A handful of cardamom, cinnamon, juniper, and peppercorns adds warmth to the broth, while a generous tablespoon of tomato paste contributes depth. With its several steps and multiple pots, this dish is certainly a project, but when done well, it is extraordinarily rich in flavor and textures.

PREP THE FISH: Fillet the fish, reserving the carcasses (or ask your fishmonger to do this—you should have 2 to 2¼ pounds/1 kg of fillets). Depending on the size, cut each fillet crosswise into 2 or 3 pieces. Wrap the fillets and refrigerate.

Make the broth: In a large soup pot, cook the fish carcasses in the olive oil over medium-high heat, stirring occasionally, until golden brown, 5 to 8 minutes. Add the wine to deglaze the pot, scraping up any golden bits that are stuck to the bottom.

Add the celery, carrots, onions, garlic, estratto, peppercorns, juniper berries, cardamom, cinnamon sticks, salt, and water to the pot. Bring to a boil, then lower the heat and simmer gently, skimming off any foam that collects on the surface of the broth, until reduced to about 2 quarts (2 L), about 1½ hours.

Pour the broth into a colander set over a clean pot (discard the solids). Set the broth aside.

Meanwhile, make the couscous: Pour one-quarter of the couscous into a wide bowl. Have ½ cup (120 ml) water at hand. Drizzle some water over the couscous and, using your hands, start rubbing the grains together to moisten them. As the grains

½ cup (120 ml) olive oil

1 teaspoon fine sea salt

½ teaspoon freshly ground black pepper

3 bay leaves

Wide strips of zest from 1 lemon

EQUIPMENT

Couscoussiera (see Resources, page 310) or large saucepan fitted with a steamer insert or fine-mesh sieve

begin to hydrate, they will start sticking together in small clumps. Continue adding more couscous and drizzles of water and keep sifting through the grains and rubbing them together until all of the couscous is moist (you may not use all of the water).

Add the onion, garlic, parsley, olive oil, salt, and pepper to the couscous and toss gently to combine.

Arrange the bay leaves and strips of lemon zest in the perforated top of the couscoussiera, then mound the seasoned couscous on top. Set the top of the couscoussiera over the bottom pot a third or half filled with water. (Alternatively, mound the bay leaves, lemon zest, and couscous in a steamer insert or a fine-mesh sieve set over a large saucepan.)

Set the contraption on the stove over high heat. Do not use the lid of the couscoussiera. Instead, stick three wooden spoons into the couscous, handle sides down, to act as vents. Once the water is boiling, lower the heat and simmer gently, stirring the couscous occasionally and changing the positions of the spoons, until the couscous is tender, about 1 hour.

When the couscous is almost ready, gently reheat the fish broth. Season to taste with salt and pepper.

Transfer the couscous to a large bowl. Pour about 3 cups (720 ml) hot fish broth over the couscous. Cover with a lid or a clean kitchen towel and let sit until the broth is fully absorbed, about 30 minutes. Once the broth is absorbed, toss gently to fluff.

Return the remaining fish broth to a gentle simmer, if necessary. Drop the reserved fish fillets into the broth and poach until opaque, 2 to 3 minutes, depending on the size of the fillets. Use a slotted spoon to transfer the fish to a plate. Pour the broth into a warmed pitcher and cover to keep warm.

To serve, place a generous scoop of couscous in the bottom of each shallow soup bowl and top with a couple of pieces of poached fish. Garnish with parsley. At the table, pass the pitcher of warm broth so that everyone can add as much as they like to their bowl.

NOTE: The broth can be made 1 day ahead, cooled completely, and refrigerated. Reheat gently over low heat before continuing with the recipe.

COUSCOUS

THE FIRST COUSCOUS CAME FROM THE NOMADIC PEOPLE OF
the Sahara and was most likely made of millet or rice, but as
it traveled across Africa and toward the north, it evolved to
being made with wheat, eventually becoming the traditional
dish of countries such as Algeria, Morocco, Tunisia, and Libya.
It is unclear exactly when couscous first appeared in Sicily, but
surprisingly enough, no mention of couscous is found from the
time of the Arab colonization, which started in the ninth century.
Couscous may have actually become more common in the
late eighteenth century, as the booming coral trade beckoned
many Trapanese laborers to the north coast of Africa, further
cementing the relationships between western Sicily and Tunisia
and Morocco.

Dried parboiled couscous has become a convenience food
for many. But taking the time to cook couscous in the traditional
way results in a much more complex taste and texture than the
instant method. Each Mediterranean country makes its couscous
slightly differently. In Sicily, coarse semolina flour is spread on a
large flat terra-cotta dish called a mafaradda, and then spritzed
with water, and massaged together until small beads of dough
form. At this point, the couscous can be steamed fresh.

To steam dried couscous in the traditional way, the couscous
first must be rehydrated. Water is rubbed into the couscous until
the grains begin to stick together in small clumps. This act is called
incocciare, from the Greek *kokkos*, meaning "nut," and indicates
how the grains should look—bumpy and ranging in size from a
sesame seed to a peppercorn. Once the couscous has been
rehydrated, it is seasoned and then steamed in a couscoussiera
(or *couscoussier* in French), a pot with holes on the bottom that
sits over another pot full of simmering water, until tender and
fluffy. (Many couscoussieras are metal, but some are made of
terra-cotta, in which case the cook may press a quick dough
of flour and water around the joint of the two vessels to ensure
that the simmering water below does not evaporate too quickly.)
The cooked couscous is then anointed with broth and set aside
to absorb it before being topped with a soup or stew. Until a few
decades ago, this practice was part of an intangible heritage
passed on from mother to daughter, but now you can find many
videos online that demonstrate it clearly.

PASTA AND RICE
pasta e riso

Sicilians hold the record for being the biggest pasta eaters in the world, with an average of 88 pounds (40 kilos) per person per year, almost twice as much as the rest of Italy. It is our daily meal—sometimes even twice a day!—and practically part of our DNA.

The long history of Italian pasta can be condensed into three key words: lagane, itryia, and spaghetti. Roman historian Marcus Gavius Apicius was the first to write about lagane, a type of lasagna noodle made of flour and water, in *De Re Coquinaria* (*On the Subject of Cooking*), the oldest known cookbook in existence. Fast-forward to Idrisi, an Arab geographer in the court of King Roger II. During the twelfth century, he witnessed the manufacture of pasta in Trabia, a small town near Palermo, where a dried pasta called itryia was produced and exported all over the Mediterranean. By his account, itryia was a long, slender noodle that closely resembled modern-day vermicelli. Fast-forward once again, this time to 1819, when the slang word *spaghetti* (meaning "small string") first appeared in the *Dizionario della lingua italiana* (*Dictionary of the Italian Language*) and became part of the official language. By this time, Italian-style pasta was becoming well known around the world.

The pastas of Southern Italy compared to those of the north illustrate two distinct worlds, ingredients, rituals, and habits. Northern pasta is most commonly pasta all'uovo, made from soft wheat and eggs, which add protein and elasticity to the dough. Pasta made south of Rome—in Sicily, Puglia, and Calabria—most often consists of just durum wheat (semolina) and water.

This results in a sturdy dough that can hold all kinds of ridged or curved shapes, ideal for collecting pools of sauce.

Many older Italians grew up with a taste for soft, slightly overcooked pasta because the pasta produced at that time could not really hold the al dente cooking that is popular today. Things started changing in the early twentieth century, when the worldwide demand for dried pasta exploded, thanks to the millions of Southern Italian immigrants who had settled in other countries. To meet this demand, Sicily stepped up its wheat production, planting modern varieties that increased the elasticity and resilience of the flour, which produced a firmer bite, a development that transformed the way people eat their pasta. As the farming processes and pasta technology improved, people came to love al dente noodles, and as dried pasta shipped out around the world, it cemented itself as a staple of Sicily's national identity.

Until the 1960s, the most common Sicilian pasta shape was maccheroni, a long noodle with a hole down the center that was made by wrapping a slender sausage of dough around a straw. Now, like so much else, maccheroni is industrially made and known as bucatini, which is still a very popular shape in Sicily, especially for pasta con le sarde (see Bucatini with Sardines and Wild Fennel, page 99). A very local variation of maccheroni is the coil-shaped busiate (see Fresh Busiate Pasta, page 93) from Trapani. Today, some of the most common dried pasta shapes in the south are short and hollow, such as shell-like cavatelli, ring-shaped anelletti, and tubular ziti.

PASTA WITH EGGPLANT AND TOMATOES

pasta alla norma

SERVES 4 TO 6

Vegetable oil, for frying

2 pounds (900 g) firm eggplant, cut into 1½-inch (4 cm) cubes

Fine sea salt

1 pound (450 g) dried ziti or other tubular pasta

3 cups (480 ml) good-quality tomato sauce, homemade (page 87) or store-bought, warmed

4 ounces (115 g) ricotta salata cheese, grated

A handful of coarsely chopped fresh basil

Stories abound about the origins of this dish—who was Norma?—but the name of this recipe most likely came long after its "invention." Indeed, pasta with tomatoes and fried eggplant is an almost intuitive combination in a place where both vegetables grow so abundantly. Mounding the fried eggplant on top of the seasoned pasta preserves its integrity—the dish naturally comes together as everyone scoops out their portion.

POUR AT LEAST 2 inches (5 cm) of vegetable oil into a wide heavy-bottomed pot and heat over medium heat until it is hot enough to fry in (see Deep-Frying, page 30). Set a wire rack in a sheet pan.

Once the oil is ready, carefully lower as many eggplant cubes as will fit without crowding into the hot oil. Fry, flipping occasionally, until golden brown all over, about 5 minutes. Use a slotted spoon to transfer the fried eggplant to the rack to drain. Sprinkle with salt. Repeat to fry the remaining eggplant cubes.

Meanwhile, in a large pot of boiling salted water, cook the pasta until al dente. Drain.

Transfer the pasta to a large serving bowl, along with the warmed sauce and half of the grated ricotta salata and half of the basil. Toss gently to combine. Pile the fried eggplant over the pasta and top with the remaining grated ricotta salata and basil. Serve at once.

PENNE WITH FRESH TOMATOES AND BASIL

penne picchio pacchio

SERVES 4

2 pounds (900 g) plum tomatoes

Fine sea salt

1 large garlic clove, coarsely chopped

1 bunch of fresh basil, leaves coarsely chopped

½ cup (120 ml) olive oil

1 pound (450 g) dried penne or other short tubular pasta

Freshly ground black pepper

Sometimes called penne pic pac, this is the easiest pasta you can imagine, made in summer when tomatoes, garlic, and basil are all at their fragrant peak. The heat of the boiled noodles and the motion of stirring all the raw ingredients together will blend the juices in the serving bowl. Letting the sauce ingredients sit and meld for an hour or two before adding the pasta will only make this more delicious. The hardest part of this recipe is finding really good tomatoes and some excellent dried pasta. Look for San Marzano or Roma tomatoes and, if possible, seek out artisanal penne (the penne from Feudo Mondello in the Belice Valley is wonderful, though finding it outside Sicily is a challenge).

BRING A POT of water to a boil. Add the tomatoes to the water and boil for 30 seconds. Use a slotted spoon to transfer the tomatoes to a bowl and let cool. Reserve the pot and cooking water for the pasta.

When the tomatoes are cool enough to handle, peel off their skins—they should slip off easily. Chop the tomatoes into large chunks. If the tomatoes are very juicy, you can put them in a colander, sprinkle with salt, and let them drain for a few minutes to get rid of the excess liquid.

Transfer the chopped tomatoes to a large serving bowl. Add the garlic, basil, and olive oil. If you haven't already salted the tomatoes, add salt to taste.

Bring the reserved cooking water back up to a boil and salt it generously. Add the penne to the boiling water and cook until al dente.

Drain the pasta and add directly to the bowl of tomatoes. Mix thoroughly, season with plenty of pepper, and serve at once.

NOTE: The raw sauce can be made 2 hours in advance and set aside at room temperature.

TOMATOES

SICILY IS KNOWN FOR ITS POMODORO SICCAGNO, DEEP RED,
full-flavored tomatoes whose name refers more to a way of
farming than a specific variety. Dry-farming—cultivating plants
without irrigation—is a method born of necessity: Some areas
of the island see only a small amount of precipitation all year,
concentrated over the winter months, which results in long
summers marked by soaring temperatures and not a drop of rain.

Traditionally, tomato seeds were sown on March 19, the
feast day of Saint Joseph, a date very close to the official start
of spring and the end of the seasonal rains. The seeds would
soak up that moisture and germinate, then be left to make their
own way, waterless, through summer. To grow in this forbidding
atmosphere, tomatoes need a clay-heavy soil and an altitude
(about 3,300 feet/1,000 m) that allows for cooler nights, during
which whatever dew collects on the plants can be stored and
used during the heat of the day. One of the best places for
this is in the foothills of the Madonie Mountains. This technique
produces a dense, intense fruit with an incomparable flavor. Any
type of plum tomato with a thick peel, such as Roma, Pizzutello,
or San Marzano, will work.

Now pomodoro siccagno has become a more extensive
crop and has been recognized by the Slow Food movement
(see Slow Food Presidia, page 210). Many growers in Valledolmo
and Villalba are growing pomodoro siccagno, but because of
the impacts of climate change, they no longer sow their seeds
in March but rather start seedlings indoors and then get small
plants in the ground in April.

During the hottest days of summer, many Sicilian households
are busy cooking down big batches of tomatoes into an
unseasoned puree. This puree is put through a mill to eliminate
seeds and skins, at which point it is called a passata. The passata
can then be seasoned and further cooked to become Everyday
Tomato Sauce (opposite). Or it can be salted and spread out on
wooden boards to dry under the August sun. The puree needs
regular stirring until it transforms into a dense, brick-colored
tomato paste known as estratto, which is used to dial up flavors,
thicken sauces, and add a flash of umami to pastas, soups, meat,
and fish.

EVERYDAY TOMATO SAUCE

salsa pronta

MAKES ABOUT 4 QUARTS (4 L)

8 pounds (3.6 kg) Roma
tomatoes

1½ cups (360 ml) water

3 large red onions, coarsely
chopped

6 garlic cloves, peeled and
left whole

4 bay leaves, preferably fresh

Leaves from 2 large bunches
of basil

¾ cup (180 ml) olive oil

1 tablespoon fine sea salt,
or to taste

1 tablespoon sugar, or to
taste

The idea of getting through winter without homemade tomato sauce is unheard of for most Sicilian households, so the end of August is a busy time as everyone makes big batches of salsa pronta that can be stored for the year. Since it is so often used as an ingredient that may be cooked further in a recipe, a good salsa pronta should be smooth, light, and fresh, not cooked to a paste. Cooks usually start with ripe San Marzano or Roma tomatoes, which are prized for their dense, pulpy flesh and rich flavor. Adding a simple pesto of basil and garlic and olive oil for the last bit of cooking keeps the sauce bright.

IN A LARGE heavy pot, combine the tomatoes, water, half of the red onions, half of the garlic cloves, and all of the bay leaves. Bring to a boil over medium-high heat, then reduce the heat, cover, and simmer until the tomatoes split, begin to break up, and eventually become a rough puree, about 40 minutes. Make sure to stir the tomatoes occasionally to keep them from sticking, and mash them gently against the side of the pot to help them break down. When the tomatoes are tender, remove the pot from the heat and let cool slightly.

Set a food mill over a clean pot. Pass the tomato mixture through the mill to separate the skins and pulp. Discard the skins.

In a food processor, combine the basil leaves and the remaining chopped onion and garlic cloves and pulse until finely chopped. Add to the pot of tomatoes, along with the olive oil. Bring to a boil, then reduce the heat and simmer, uncovered, until the mixture has thickened slightly, about 30 minutes. Remove from the heat and stir in the salt and sugar.

NOTE: The sauce can be used right away or bottled or frozen for later use. Sauce that has been safely processed will keep for up to 1 year stored in a cool, dark place. (For more information on canning, visit the website of the National Center for Home Food Preservation at nchfp.uga.edu.) Frozen sauce will keep for up to 3 months.

PASTA WITH TRAPANESE PESTO

paccheri con pesto trapanese

SERVES 4 TO 6

4 cups (80 g) loosely packed fresh basil leaves

1 cup (240 ml) olive oil

1 large garlic clove, coarsely chopped

Fine sea salt

1 cup (150 g) skin-on almonds, blanched and peeled

1 medium tomato, peeled and chopped

1 pound (450 g) Fresh Busiate Pasta (page 93) or Fresh Cavatelli (page 96)

Trapanese pesto is a summery sauce best made when tomatoes are in season, almonds are ready to be harvested, and the lovely red garlic from Nubia is plump and juicy. To blanch the almonds for this recipe, simply drop them in a pot of boiling water for a minute or two, then drain. When the almonds are just cool enough to handle, the peels should slip off easily.

IN A FOOD processor, combine the basil, olive oil, garlic, and 1 teaspoon salt and puree until very smooth. Add the almonds and pulse until coarsely chopped. Transfer the pesto to a large bowl and stir in the tomato.

In a large pot of boiling salted water, cook the pasta until al dente. Drain the pasta and add to the bowl of pesto, mixing quickly to preserve the pesto's freshness and bright color. Serve at once.

BUSIATE WITH BOTTARGA

busiate con bottarga

SERVES 4 TO 6

3½ ounces (100 g) bottarga
(see Resources, page 310)

1 small garlic clove

1 lemon

1 orange

¼ cup (60 ml) lukewarm
water, plus more as needed

4 tablespoons olive oil

½ teaspoon ground
cinnamon

¼ teaspoon crushed red
pepper flakes

¼ teaspoon freshly ground
black pepper

Fine sea salt

1 pound 5 ounces (600 g)
Fresh Busiate Pasta (opposite)
or other coiled fresh pasta

¼ cup (5 g) chopped fresh
flat-leaf parsley and/or mint,
for garnish

Bottarga is fish roe that has been cured under salt until it
becomes a crumbly block suitable for grating over pasta
or bread. It has a salty, deeply meaty flavor. Traditionally,
bottarga was made of red tuna roe in Sicily, while muggine
(mullet) roe is used in Sardinia. The two are very different—the
mullet is sweeter and deeper in flavor, while the tuna is more
intensely salty. Now that red tuna is endangered, most of the
Sicilian bottarga is made of yellowfin. The coast of Sicily was
once dotted with tonnare, towers that marked areas of tuna
fishing with factories for breaking down and preserving the
fish. The man in charge of curing the roe was called the *mastro
salatore*, the "salt curing expert." Tonnare are no longer active
in Sicily, and as red tuna has become endangered, so has the
future of this tradition and occupation.

Bottarga is now made in only a few places around the
island. If you find super fresh, bright pink bottarga, slice it
thinly like prosciutto and eat it with warm bread, drizzled
with good olive oil. Or make this recipe, in which finely grated
bottarga is whisked together with fresh citrus juice and olive
oil to make a light, creamy sauce for fresh coils of pasta.

USE A MICROPLANE to finely grate the bottarga, garlic, and zest
of the lemon and the orange into a large serving bowl. Gradually
whisk in the water, followed by 2 tablespoons of the olive oil.
Add the cinnamon, pepper flakes, and black pepper and whisk
to combine. Juice the lemon and orange. While whisking, add
2 tablespoons lemon juice and ¼ cup (60 ml) orange juice. The
sauce should be very creamy. If not, whisk in a little more water,
1 tablespoon at a time. Season lightly with salt.

Bring a large pot of salted water to a boil. Add the busiate and
cook until al dente. Drain the pasta, transfer to the serving bowl
with the bottarga sauce, and toss to combine, adding the remaining
2 tablespoons olive oil. Scatter the fresh herbs over the pasta and
serve at once.

FRESH BUSIATE PASTA

busiate

MAKES ABOUT 1 POUND
5 OUNCES (600 G)
FRESH PASTA

2½ cups (400 g) semolina
flour, plus more for dusting

¾ to 1 cup (180 to 240 ml)
water

EQUIPMENT
Bamboo skewer or other
long, thin rod

Busiate is the most typical pasta shape from the northwest coast of Sicily, between Trapani and Mazara del Vallo. Similar to cavatelli (see page 96), it is made from just water and semolina, but it is shaped by rolling pieces of dough around a buso, or thin wooden stick, to form a long coil. Bamboo skewers or knitting needles also work well. It takes a few tries to get the hang of making it, but you'll be rewarded with a satisfying, one-of-a-kind shape. Good-quality dried busiate is also widely available in Sicily. Busiate is the traditional pasta to serve with Trapanese Pesto (page 90) in summer, but it's equally good with a garlicky tangle of wild chicories in winter or tossed with a sauce of grated bottarga and citrus (opposite).

IN A MEDIUM bowl, mix together the semolina and water until well combined, then turn out onto a clean work surface and knead until the mixture comes together in a stiff but smooth, slightly springy dough. Cover the dough with a clean kitchen towel and let it rest for 1 hour.

Line a baking sheet with a clean kitchen towel and dust it with semolina.

Pinch off a small piece of dough and roll it with your hands on a work surface to form a long, thin rope about half the width of a pencil (about ⅛ inch/3 mm). Cut the rope into segments 8 inches (20 cm) long. (Keep the rest of the dough covered as you work to prevent it from drying out.)

Place a bamboo skewer diagonally at one end of the rope and roll it away from you so that the dough wraps tightly around the skewer, forming a corkscrew shape. Roll the pasta-wrapped skewer under your palms to flatten the dough slightly. Gently slide the pasta off the skewer. Transfer the busiate to the prepared baking sheet, dust them lightly with semolina, and repeat the rolling process to shape the rest of the dough.

To help them hold their shape while cooking, let the busiate dry for about 30 minutes at room temperature before cooking in boiling salted water.

NOTE: Fresh busiate can be made up to 2 hours ahead.

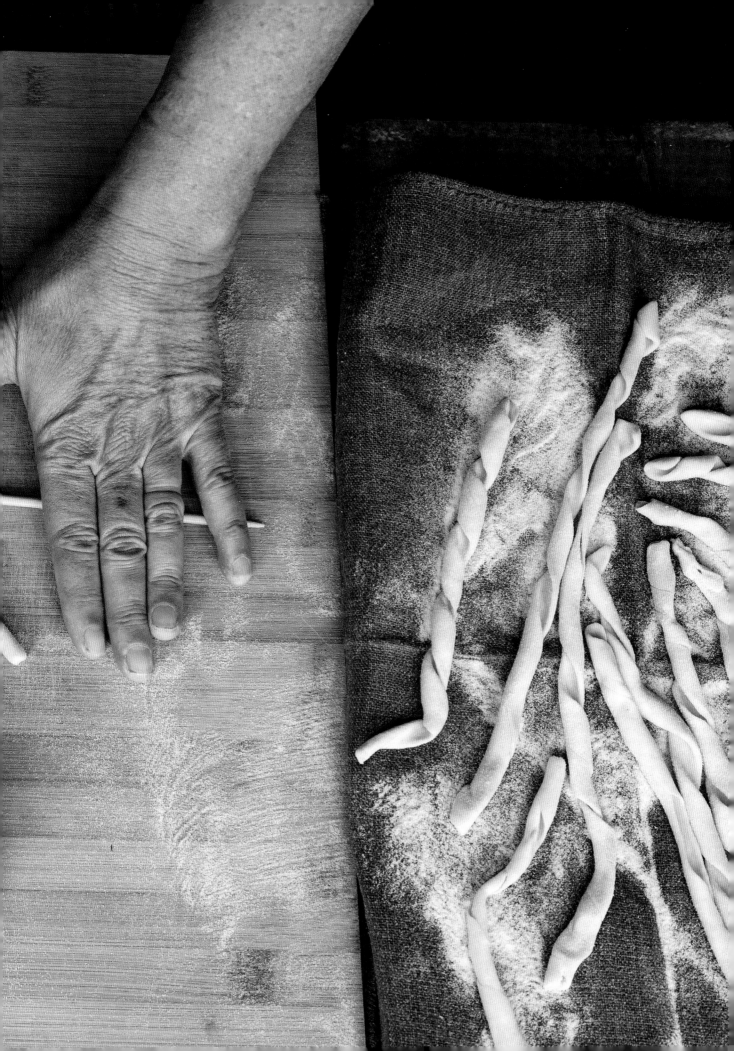

FRESH CAVATELLI

cavatelli

MAKES ABOUT 1 POUND (450 G) FRESH PASTA

2 cups (320 g) semolina flour, plus more for dusting

6 to 10 tablespoons (90 to 150 ml) water

EQUIPMENT

Ridged wooden pasta board, also sold as a gnocchi board (see Resources, page 310)

Cavatelli's name comes from the word *cavare*, which means "to carve away," and its cupped shape is ideal for collecting pools of sauce. It is a typical Southern Italian pasta made with just durum wheat and water—no eggs, no salt, no oil. The cavatelli are shaped by pushing a nub of stiff dough against a ridged wooden paddle, but if you don't have one, simply use the tines of a fork or shape the pasta against a plain wooden board or your countertop. This sturdy, chewy shape is a delicious vehicle for Trapanese Pesto (page 90) or Tuna Ragù (page 154).

IN A MEDIUM bowl (or on a clean work surface), make a mound of the semolina and make a well in the center. Pour 6 tablespoons (90 ml) of the water into the well and use your hands to mix together into a dough. If the dough is still too floury and won't come together, add more water, 1 tablespoon at a time, until it does. Knead the dough into a smooth ball; the dough will be stiff. Cover with plastic wrap and let rest at room temperature for about 30 minutes.

Line a baking sheet with a clean kitchen towel and dust it with semolina.

Cut off a piece of dough and roll it into a log about the width of your finger (keep the rest of the dough covered as you work to prevent it from drying out). Cut the log crosswise into ½-inch (1 cm) pieces. Working with one piece of dough at a time, place it on the ridged pasta paddle and use your thumb to press and roll the dough away from you in one smooth motion, which will create a small shell-shaped pasta that is ridged on the outside. (If you don't have a pasta board, simply roll the dough away from you on the tines of a fork.)

Place the shaped cavatelli on the prepared baking sheet and dust them with semolina. To help them hold their shape while cooking, let the cavatelli dry for 30 minutes to 2 hours at room temperature before cooking in boiling salted water.

NOTE: Fresh cavatelli can be made up to 2 hours ahead.

BUCATINI WITH SARDINES AND WILD FENNEL

bucatini con le sarde e finocchietto selvatico

SERVES 4 TO 6

FOR THE SAUCE

Fine sea salt

1 pound (450 g) wild fennel (see page 101), fronds trimmed

1 pound (450 g) very fresh sardines, scaled, gutted, boned, tails and heads removed

Semolina flour

1 medium onion, finely chopped

1 garlic clove, smashed

¼ cup (60 ml) olive oil

1 tablespoon estratto (sun-dried tomato paste; see Resources, page 310) or other good-quality tomato paste

½ cup (120 ml) white wine

½ cup (65 g) pine nuts

½ cup (65 g) raisins

3 cups (720 ml) good-quality tomato sauce, homemade (page 87) or store-bought

Freshly ground black pepper

FOR THE BREAD CRUMB TOPPING

1¾ cups (215 g) plain dried bread crumbs

¼ cup (60 ml) olive oil

2 tablespoons sugar

1 garlic clove, smashed

Pinch of fine sea salt

Pinch of crushed red pepper flakes

A huge variety of dishes and cuisines exists within Sicily, but pasta con le sarde is one that you can find almost anywhere on the island. Of course, there are variations: In Catania, cooks use small anchovies called masculini in place of sardines. In mountainous areas, where fresh sardines are hard to come by, you'll find a similar but vegetarian dish whose name, *pasta con le sarde a mare*, means "pasta with the sardines out to sea"! But the concept of a saucy mixture made with lots of wild fennel, tomato sauce, raisins, and pine nuts remains. It is a potent combination that almost completely conceals the flavor of the sardines, a trait that helps illustrate the complicated relationship Sicilians have long had with fish.

MAKE THE SAUCE: Bring a large pot of salted water to a boil. Add the fennel and cook until tender, about 20 minutes. Using tongs, transfer the fennel to a colander to drain and cool for a few minutes, then finely chop it. (Keep the pot and water for cooking the pasta.)

Depending on how many people you are serving, place 4 to 6 of the cleaned sardines on a small plate and coat them on both sides with semolina. Set aside for the fried sardine garnish.

In a large pan, sauté the onion and garlic in the olive oil over medium heat until golden, 2 to 3 minutes. Dissolve the estratto in the wine, then add it to the pan along with the chopped fennel, pine nuts, raisins, tomato sauce, and the remaining (uncoated) sardines. Sprinkle with salt and black pepper and simmer until the sardines break up and are cooked through, about 10 minutes.

Make the bread crumb topping: In a small skillet over medium heat, combine the bread crumbs, olive oil, sugar, garlic, salt, and pepper flakes. Cook, stirring constantly to prevent the bread crumbs from burning, until they are crisp and golden brown, 3 to 5 minutes. Transfer the toasted bread crumbs to a bowl and stir in the chopped parsley.

ingredients and recipe continue

¼ cup (5 g) chopped fresh
flat-leaf parsley

**FOR THE FRIED SARDINE
GARNISH AND ASSEMBLY**
Olive oil, for frying

1 pound (450 g) dried
bucatini or other long pasta

Make the fried sardine garnish: Line a plate with paper towels.
Return the skillet you used for toasting the bread crumbs to
medium heat. Pour in a splash of olive oil and, once it's hot, add
the semolina-coated sardines. Fry them, turning once, until they're
cooked through, about 3 minutes. Transfer to the paper towels to
drain.

Assemble the dish: Bring the fennel cooking water in the pot to
a boil. Add the bucatini and cook until almost al dente. Reserving
a ladle or two of the cooking water, drain the pasta and transfer
it directly to the pan of sauce. Toss gently to coat the pasta in the
sauce, adding some of the reserved pasta water to thin the sauce as
needed. Remove from the heat.

To serve, scatter the toasted bread crumbs over the pasta and
garnish each plate with a fried sardine. Serve at once.

WILD FENNEL

WITH ITS SWEET ANISE FLAVOR, WILD FENNEL (FINOCCHIETTO selvatico) is one of the most distinctive ingredients in Sicilian food and central to many classic dishes, including its most iconic: Bucatini with Sardines and Wild Fennel (page 99). Its tender stalks and feathery fronds may be made into fritters, used to season soups, sautéed with tomato sauce as a side dish, or served as a salad, dressed with oil and vinegar. Domesticated fennel, with its round white bulb and chalky, inedible stalks, has little to do with the wild variety and cannot be substituted for it.

In winter, hardy finocchietto selvatico grows wild all over the island, its bright green fronds lining the roads and carpeting the hills. In February and March, you'll see small armies of foragers picking wild fennel, either for their own use or to sell at market. Foragers prefer the most remote, mountainous areas of Sicily because the cooler air keeps the plant from bolting too quickly. Also, the first rule of a good forager is to pick plants far off the beaten (and polluted!) path.

Since fresh wild fennel is available for such a short period, most households like to stock up. After a good washing, the plant is laboriously trimmed down to the most tender parts and blanched in boiling salted water. The drained greens are divided into bags and frozen, to be used all year.

In summer, the plant forms yellow umbrella-shaped flowers. Around September, the seeds can be harvested from the dried flowers; their anise bite makes a fragrant addition to sausages and breads. Unlike the seeds, wild fennel pollen is not commonly used in Sicily outside of a few trendy restaurants, despite its popularity elsewhere around the world. Finocchietto selvatico defies cultivation, but its seeds have nonetheless traveled with Sicilian immigrants all over the world, and you will find it growing wild in certain temperate climates, including coastal California, where it is considered an invasive pest in some areas.

Unfortunately, there is no real substitute for wild fennel in a recipe, especially when a large quantity is called for. When just a small amount is needed, you may substitute equal parts fresh dill and parsley, but the flavor will be quite different. Likewise, a small handful of dried fennel seeds can give a hint of the elusive, licorice-like note typical of wild fennel.

RAISINS AND PINE NUTS

COMMONLY PAIRED WITH ONE ANOTHER IN SICILIAN FOOD,
raisins and pine nuts show up in many recipes, including Bucatini
with Cauliflower, Pine Nuts, and Raisins (opposite) and Sardines
Stuffed with Bread Crumbs and Raisins (page 133). The duo is
often combined with bread crumbs for stuffing meat, fish, and
vegetables, such as zucchini, peppers, or eggplants. The grapes
most commonly turned into raisins here are known as uvetta di
Corinto. These little black seedless grapes are also known for
giving structure and body to Malvasia, a sweet wine from the
Aeolian Islands. Drying the grapes is quite a process, and it was
the greatest industry of the Aeolian Islands until the phylloxera
insect wiped out most of the grapes in the late 1800s.

The uvetta di Corinto has a hint of acidity that works very
well with the nutty sweetness of pine nuts. Extremely common
in both sweet and savory recipes in Sicily, pine nuts are hardly
ever toasted here. Unfortunately, the labor cost to produce raisins
and pine nuts has become so prohibitive that most raisins are
imported from Morocco, while the Sicilian market is saturated
with pine nuts from Turkey and China.

BUCATINI WITH CAULIFLOWER, PINE NUTS, AND RAISINS

bucatini con broccolo arriminato

SERVES 4 TO 6

FOR THE SAUCE

Fine sea salt

1 head cauliflower (about 2 pounds/900 g), cut into bite-size florets

1 medium red onion, chopped

⅓ cup (80 ml) olive oil

3 oil-packed anchovy fillets

3 tablespoons pine nuts

3 tablespoons raisins, soaked in hot water for 5 minutes

1 tablespoon estratto (sun-dried tomato paste; see Resources, page 310) or other good-quality tomato paste

1 cup (240 ml) white wine

Freshly ground black pepper

FOR THE TOASTED BREAD CRUMBS

½ cup (60 g) plain dried bread crumbs

1 tablespoon olive oil

1 tablespoon finely chopped fresh flat-leaf parsley

FOR ASSEMBLY

1 pound (450 g) dried bucatini or other long pasta

Bucatini is one of the favorite pastas of Sicily, and it is the classic choice to accompany this rich, slowly cooked cauliflower sauce. Pine nuts, dried raisins, and the acidity of white wine balance the creaminess of this sauce.

MAKE THE SAUCE: Bring a large pot of salted water to a boil. Add the cauliflower and cook until tender when poked with a fork, about 10 minutes. Use a slotted spoon to transfer the cauliflower to a colander. Reserve 2 cups (480 ml) of the cooking water. (Keep the pot with the remaining water to cook the pasta, adding more water if needed.)

In a large skillet, sauté the onion in the olive oil over medium heat until very light golden, 2 to 3 minutes. Add the anchovies, mashing them with a wooden spoon, then stir in the pine nuts, raisins, and cooked cauliflower.

Dissolve the estratto in the wine, then pour the mixture into the pan along with the reserved 2 cups of cauliflower cooking water. Simmer gently until the cauliflower is falling-apart tender, 30 to 40 minutes. Season to taste with salt and pepper. Keep warm over very low heat.

Meanwhile, make the toasted bread crumbs: In a small skillet, cook the bread crumbs in the olive oil over medium heat, stirring constantly, until well toasted, about 3 minutes. Remove from the heat and stir in the parsley.

Assemble the dish: Return the pot of salted water to a boil. Add the bucatini and cook until al dente. Reserving 2 cups (480 ml) of the cooking water, drain the pasta in a colander. Transfer the pasta to the pan of cauliflower. Toss gently to coat the pasta in the sauce, adding a little cooking water if needed.

Scatter the toasted bread crumbs on top and serve at once.

PASTA WITH SAUSAGE AND BROCCOLI

pasta con salsiccia e sparacelli

SERVES 4 TO 6

Fine sea salt

1 pound (750 g) broccoli or broccolini

6 tablespoons (90 ml) olive oil, plus more as needed

⅓ cup (35 g) skin-on almonds, blanched and peeled (see page 90)

Freshly ground black pepper

12 ounces (340 g) uncooked Italian fennel sausage

1 cup (240 ml) white wine

1 medium yellow onion, finely chopped

2 garlic cloves, finely chopped

1 pound (450 g) dried pasta, such as busiate, fusilli, rigatoni, or penne rigate

Thinly shaved ricotta salata cheese, for serving

Pork sausage is available at any butcher shop in Sicily, usually seasoned simply with salt, pepper, and wild fennel seeds. Broccoli is known as sparacelli in Sicily. When they are cooked together, their meatiness and bitterness meld with a splash of white wine to make a wholly satisfying meal.

BRING A POT of lightly salted water to a boil. While the water heats up, trim the broccoli, discarding any tough, woody ends. Cut off the florets and set them aside. Cut the stems and any tender leaves into bite-size pieces.

First, add just the stems to the boiling water and cook until they are just tender, about 2 minutes. Add the florets and leaves to the boiling water and cook until they turn bright green, 1 to 2 minutes. Use a slotted spoon to transfer all of the broccoli to a colander. (Reserve the pot and the cooking water for the sauce and the pasta.)

In a food processor, combine the broccoli, 3 tablespoons of the olive oil, the almonds, a pinch each of salt and pepper, and ¼ cup (60 ml) of the reserved cooking water. Puree until smooth. If it's too thick to blend, add another splash of cooking water and a drizzle of oil. Taste and season with salt and pepper. Set aside.

In a large heavy skillet, cook the sausage in 1 tablespoon of the olive oil over high heat, breaking it up with a spoon, until it is starting to brown, about 8 minutes. Transfer it to a bowl and set aside.

Return the skillet to medium heat. Pour in ½ cup (120 ml) of the wine and simmer for about 1 minute, scraping the bottom of the skillet with a wooden spoon to deglaze the pan, and then pour the pan juices over the browned sausage in the bowl.

Return the skillet to medium heat and cook the onion in the remaining 2 tablespoons olive oil until softened, about 5 minutes. Add the garlic and cook, stirring constantly, for 30 seconds. Stir in the sausage along with its juices and the remaining ½ cup (120 ml) wine. Simmer for about 15 minutes, adding a splash of broccoli cooking water if the mixture starts to stick to the pan.

Meanwhile, top up the pot of cooking water as needed and bring to a boil. Add the pasta and cook until al dente.

Reserving 1 cup (240 ml) of the cooking water, drain the pasta and add to the skillet with the sausage. Pour in the broccoli mixture, increase the heat to high, and toss gently to coat the pasta in the sauce, adding a little cooking water if needed to lighten the sauce.

To serve, divide the pasta among shallow bowls and top with some thinly shaved ricotta salata.

SPAGHETTI WITH ANCHOVIES AND TOASTED BREAD CRUMBS

pasta con acciuga e mollica

SERVES 4

6 to 8 oil-packed anchovy fillets

½ cup (120 ml) olive oil, plus more for drizzling

2 garlic cloves, peeled and left whole

1 heaping tablespoon estratto (sun-dried tomato paste; see Resources, page 310) or other good-quality tomato paste

Pinch of crushed red pepper flakes

1 cup (125 g) plain dried bread crumbs

Finely grated zest of 1 lemon

½ teaspoon ground cinnamon

Fine sea salt and freshly ground black pepper

1 pound (450 g) dried spaghetti or other long pasta

2 tablespoons chopped fresh flat-leaf parsley, for garnish

A dish very typical of Palermo, this recipe is called pasta *ca a muddica atturrata*—which means pasta "with toasted bread crumbs"—in dialect. Its depth comes from a spoonful of estratto (sun-dried tomato paste) and a few anchovies that are melted in plenty of olive oil. As with all deceptively basic recipes, balance is key—cinnamon, fresh lemon zest, and a pinch of red pepper flakes help keep the extreme umaminess of the anchovies and tomato paste in check. This is a great weeknight pantry pasta, and it's so good that you'll want to make sure you always have the ingredients on hand.

IN A MEDIUM saucepan, cook the anchovies in the olive oil over medium-low heat, crushing them with a wooden spoon until they dissolve. Add the garlic cloves and cook until golden, 3 to 5 minutes. Mix in the tomato paste, smearing it in the pan with the spoon until it is completely incorporated into the oil. Reduce the heat to low and cook, stirring occasionally, until all the flavors have melded together, 10 to 15 minutes. Stir in the pepper flakes and remove the pan from the heat.

While the anchovy sauce is cooking, in a large dry skillet, toast the bread crumbs over medium heat, stirring constantly so they do not burn, until they are golden and smell toasted, 4 to 5 minutes. Add the lemon zest and cinnamon. Season with salt and black pepper and remove from the heat.

Bring a large pot of lightly salted water to a boil. (The anchovies in the sauce already contribute a good amount of saltiness.) Add the spaghetti and cook until al dente. Reserving 1 cup (240 ml) of the cooking water, drain the pasta and return the noodles to the pot. Add the anchovy sauce, half of the toasted bread crumbs, and a splash of the reserved cooking water. Stir to combine, adding more cooking water if the sauce doesn't easily cloak the noodles. Transfer the pasta to a serving dish and top with the rest of the bread crumbs, the parsley, and a healthy drizzle of olive oil. Serve at once.

RAVIOLI FILLED WITH RICOTTA AND MINT

ravioli ricotta e menta

SERVES 4 TO 6

1⅔ cups (200 g) all-purpose flour, plus more for dusting

1¼ cups (200 g) semolina flour

3 large eggs

1¾ cups (440 g) whole-milk ricotta cheese

2 tablespoons freshly grated Parmigiano-Reggiano cheese, plus more for serving

½ cup (10 g) finely chopped fresh mint leaves

Pinch of freshly grated nutmeg

Pinch of ground cinnamon

Pinch of crushed red pepper flakes

Fine sea salt

3 cups (720 ml) good-quality tomato sauce, homemade (page 87) or store-bought, warmed

EQUIPMENT
Pasta machine

Large ravioli stuffed with ricotta and mint is a typical dish on Pantelleria, the large volcanic island that floats between Sicily and North Africa. Historically, every time a new calf was born, the cow's owner would make ricotta from the milk and stuff it into ravioli, both as a celebration and as a wish for continued good luck. Usually served with tomato sauce, these ravioli are equally delicious with melted butter seasoned with sage leaves.

IN A MEDIUM bowl, combine the all-purpose flour and semolina flour, then make a well in the center and crack the eggs into it. Use a fork to stir the eggs while gradually incorporating flour from the sides. When the mixture becomes too stiff to stir, transfer it to a clean work surface and knead to form a smooth ball. Cover with plastic wrap and set aside to rest while you make the filling.

In another bowl, mix together the ricotta, Parmigiano, mint, nutmeg, cinnamon, and pepper flakes. Season to taste with salt.

After the dough has rested, cut it into 8 equal portions. Working with 1 portion at a time, pass the dough through a pasta machine set to the thickest setting. Change the machine to the next thinner setting. Pass the dough through again. Continue decreasing the machine's setting and passing the dough through until you've rolled the dough through the second-thinnest setting. Repeat the rolling process with the other dough pieces.

Lay out a pasta sheet on a lightly floured work surface. Place small spoonfuls of the filling every few inches along one long side of the dough. Fold the dough over the filling and press the edges with your fingertips to seal. Trim the dough with a small knife or a round cutter to form filled pasta squares or rounds. Repeat with all the dough sheets and remaining filling, arranging the ravioli in a single layer on lightly floured baking sheets as you work. Let the ravioli dry for 30 minutes to 1 hour before cooking.

Bring a large pot of salted water to a boil. Add the ravioli to the boiling water and cook until tender, about 6 minutes. Use a slotted spoon to transfer the ravioli to a large serving platter and spoon the sauce over them. Top with grated Parmigiano-Reggiano. Serve at once.

NOTE: Uncooked ravioli can be frozen for up to 1 month. Freeze them in a single layer on a floured baking sheet until firm, then transfer to a sealable plastic bag or container and store in the freezer. Do not thaw before cooking.

SICILIAN CHEESES

SICILY IS A SMALL CONTINENT UNTO ITSELF, ESPECIALLY WHEN it comes to cheese production. The animal's breed, the diverse vegetation that it feeds upon, the herder's expertise—all of these factors can be considered very special "ingredients" that contribute to the variety and quality of Sicilian cheeses.

When you leave the big cities and start driving through the countryside, you will almost certainly bump into a flock of sheep blocking the road, their chorus of twinkling bells and *baas* filling the air. Looking up into the hills, you might see a few cows placidly grazing in their rocky pastures. Two types of cow fit particularly well into this landscape—the huge, black Cinisara, which comes from the town of Cinisi west of Palermo, and the Razza Modicana, a sturdy cow with a furry, reddish-brown coat from the area around Modica. Over hundreds of years, both breeds have grown to thrive on the island's harsh, thorny land, and they are cherished for their milk, which is made into excellent cheeses. The Razza Modicana is capable of producing over 20 quarts (20 L) a day of the richest-quality milk, which goes into making Ragusano DOP, also known as caciocavallo, the best cheese from Ragusa and possibly all of Sicily. Shaped like a stepping-stone, this firm, golden cheese gets decidedly more piquant as it ages.

The two best-known native sheep breeds are the Beliciana, from the Belice Valley in western Sicily, and the Comisana, from the area around Comiso in the southeast. While the animals' wool was once woven into carpets and coats, more attention is now focused on the milk that they so generously provide, which goes into making excellent pecorino, tuma, primo sale, and ricotta (for more on ricotta, see page 294). The fresh, unsalted curds are known as tuma and must be eaten quickly; tuma's soft, snow-white mass has a pleasant squeak to it. If the curds are salted and allowed to age in a cool spot for a week, the result is *primo sale* ("first salt"). Peppercorns or coriander seeds are often folded into the curds before they are salted, adding little pops of heat and spice. Sold in groceries, primo sale is greatly appreciated by Sicilians for its mild flavor and texture. With several more months of aging, primo sale transforms into its most recognizable form: crumbly, pungent pecorino.

Both pecorino and Ragusano are used for cooking, as a baked cheese, and for filling focaccia, as well as grating on

pasta in place of Parmigiano. Variations on these two main cheeses are found throughout Sicily. Cow's-milk provola can come from either the Nebrodi or Madonie Mountains. The bright yellow Piacentino Ennese, a sheep's-milk cheese made in Enna, gets its incredible color from saffron pistils. Maiorchino is one of the most ancient types of pecorino from the northeast area of Sicily and is eaten mostly as a table cheese.

A few decades ago, the Girgentana, a beautiful breed of goat with long, curly horns, was rescued from the brink of extinction by a man named Giacomo Gatì. He not only saved the breed but also started producing wonderful chèvre-style cheeses that have only recently started to become popular in Sicily. Before Gatì, goat's milk was not widely used, and while goat meat might have been eaten for Easter, it was much less prized than lamb. Gatì has also successfully experimented with using vegetarian rennet, from artichokes and cardoons, for making some of his cheeses.

ANELLETTI TIMBALLO
timballo di anelletti

SERVES 10

1 medium onion, finely chopped

1 carrot, finely chopped

1 celery stalk, finely chopped

¼ cup (60 ml) olive oil

8 ounces (225 g) ground meat, preferably a mixture of pork and beef or veal

1 tablespoon estratto (sun-dried tomato paste; see Resources, page 310) or other good-quality tomato paste

½ cup (120 ml) white wine

6 cups (1.5 L) good-quality tomato sauce, homemade (page 87) or store-bought

1 cup (150 g) frozen peas

Fine sea salt and freshly ground black pepper

Vegetable oil, for frying

1 large eggplant, peeled and cut crosswise into slices ¼ inch (6 mm) thick

2 pounds (900 g) dried anelletti (ring-shaped pasta)

¼ cup (30 g) grated Parmigiano-Reggiano cheese

Softened butter, for the cake pan

⅔ cup (80 g) plain dried bread crumbs

5 ounces (140 g) thinly sliced prosciutto cotto or cooked ham

3½ ounces (100 g) thinly sliced caciocavallo, provola, or low-moisture mozzarella cheese

Found mainly in Sicily, the little ring-shaped pasta known as anelletti is very sturdy and difficult to overcook, which is important in the case of this recipe. The anelletti are first boiled and then baked around a stuffing of rich ragù, cheese, ham, and eggplant, and through those two cookings should still retain some bite. This timballo is definitely a celebratory dish and calls for a big table of friends and family to eat it, though Palermitans have also been known to tote it on a picnic or to the beach (still in its pan!), where it can be snacked upon between dips in the sea.

IN A LARGE deep skillet, cook the onion, carrot, and celery in the olive oil over medium-high heat until softened, about 5 minutes. Add the ground meat and cook, stirring occasionally, until browned, about 5 minutes.

Dissolve the estratto in the wine, add to the meat mixture, and cook until nearly evaporated. Add 4 cups (1 L) of the tomato sauce and the peas. Bring to a boil, then reduce the heat and simmer gently, uncovered, stirring occasionally, until reduced and thickened, about 45 minutes. Remove from the heat and season with salt and pepper. Set the ragù aside.

Meanwhile, pour at least 2 inches (5 cm) of vegetable oil into a wide heavy-bottomed pan and heat over medium heat until it is hot enough to fry in (see Deep-Frying, page 30). Line a large plate with paper towels.

Once the oil is ready, deep-fry the eggplant in batches until golden brown on both sides, about 4 minutes per batch. Transfer to the paper towels and set aside to cool.

Bring a large pot of salted water to a boil. Add the pasta and cook until just al dente (it will cook further in the oven). Drain the pasta well and return it to the pot. Stir in the Parmigiano and remaining 2 cups (480 ml) tomato sauce.

Preheat the oven to 350°F (180°C). Butter a 12-inch (30 cm) round cake pan and coat it with the bread crumbs; tap out the excess and save for scattering over the filled timballo.

Line the bottom and sides of the prepared pan with a layer of pasta 1 inch (2.5 cm) thick (reserve the remaining pasta for the top). Arrange the slices of eggplant evenly over the pasta base, followed by the prosciutto cotto. Spoon the ragù over the ham, then top with the slices of cheese, leaving enough room for another thick layer

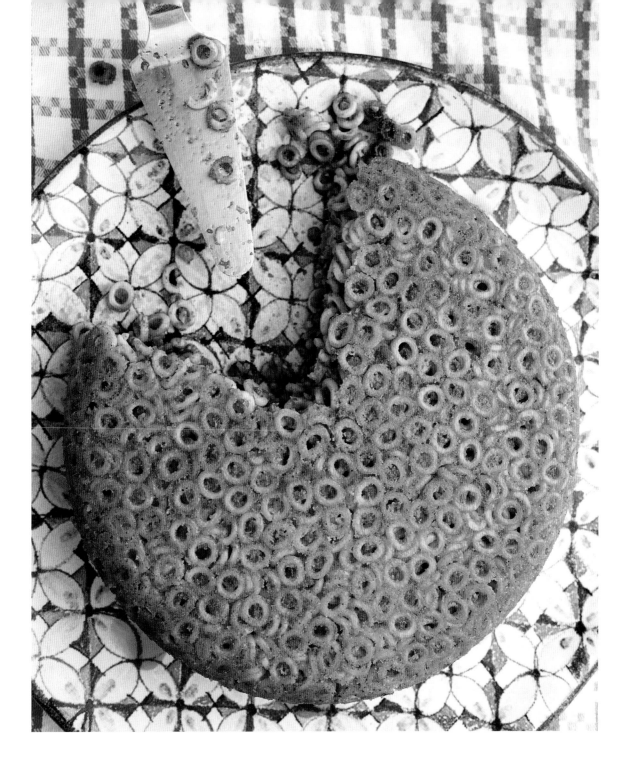

of pasta. Spread the remaining pasta on top to seal in the filling ingredients, smoothing the top. Sprinkle the remaining bread crumbs on top.

Bake until the top of the timballo is golden brown and the pasta feels set, about 50 minutes. Remove the timballo from the oven and let rest for at least 15 minutes before inverting onto a serving plate. Serve warm or at room temperature.

NOTE: The timballo can be baked up to 3 hours in advance. Leftovers can be reheated in a warm oven or microwave.

BORAGE RISOTTO

risotto di borragine

SERVES 4

Fine sea salt

12 ounces (340 g) cleaned borage leaves

1 small onion, finely chopped

2 tablespoons olive oil

1½ cups (300 g) risotto rice, such as Carnaroli, Arborio, or Vialone Nano

¼ cup (60 ml) white wine

½ cup (60 g) grated Piacentino Ennese (see Resources, page 310) or pecorino cheese, plus more for garnish

¼ cup (30 g) grated Parmigiano-Reggiano cheese

Borage flowers (optional), for garnish

As soon as the temperature starts to rise at the end of winter, borage's furry leaves pop up all over Sicily's gardens and fields. The hearty-looking herb has a surprisingly delicate, cucumber-like taste, and this verdant risotto looks as much like spring as it tastes of it. To preserve its bright color and flavor (and to soften the tiny, nettle-like needles that cover the plant), the borage should always be blanched first and then added to the dish toward the end of cooking. As a final touch, the risotto is garnished with a grating of saffron-tinted Piacentino Ennese cheese (though pecorino also works well) and a handful of bright blue borage flowers.

BRING A LARGE pot of salted water to a boil. Add the borage and cook until softened but still bright green, about 3 minutes. Using tongs, transfer the borage to a colander. (Reserve the cooking liquid over low heat for making the risotto.) Place the borage in a bowl. Using an immersion blender (or a food processor), puree the borage until very smooth. Set aside.

In a heavy-bottomed saucepan, cook the onion in the olive oil over medium heat, stirring occasionally, until softened and translucent, 6 to 8 minutes. Add the rice and cook for a minute or two, stirring to coat it with the olive oil. Add the white wine and cook, stirring occasionally, until it has been absorbed by the rice.

Stir about 1 cup (240 ml) of the hot cooking liquid into the rice and cook, stirring frequently, until the rice is almost dry. Continue adding the cooking liquid, about 1 cup (240 ml) at a time, stirring frequently and letting it simmer until the rice is creamy and just al dente (you will most likely not use all of the liquid). Stir in the borage puree when the rice is almost tender.

When the risotto is ready, stir in the grated cheeses and, if necessary, season with salt.

Serve right away, garnished with more of the grated cheese and the borage blossoms (if using).

CITRUS

THE CHRISTMAS SEASON IN SICILY IS SYNONYMOUS WITH citrus—dense groves of blood orange, lemon, and mandarin trees, first punctuated with waxy, bright white blossoms, then laden with bright orange and yellow fruits, the magical scent of their essential oils filling the air. Citrus needs cool temperatures and protection from the wind in order to thrive, and citrus groves fill the plains around Catania and Palermo, as well as the northern coastline between Palermo and Messina.

The Arabs introduced citrus to Sicily and planted gardens that included bitter oranges and lemons, mainly for decorative purposes. The second wave of sweet oranges arrived much later, in the 1600s, thanks to Portuguese explorers. These oranges are called Portogalli, meaning from Portugal, by market vendors.

The citrus industry exploded in Sicily in the 1800s, and now Sicily and Calabria together are responsible for more than 80 percent of all citrus production in Italy. The most popular hybrids grown in Sicily are tangerines, Sanguinello, and Tarocco. The conca d'oro, or Golden Basin, surrounding Palermo is renowned for its mandarin orchards—specifically the mandarino di Ciaculli, now a Slow Food Presidium (see page 210)—while the area surrounding Catania is ideal for producing blood oranges. The soil quality, abundant water, and dramatic daily temperature changes are what a blood orange requires to get its deep color. Small orchards dot the area around Ribera, where the Ribera orange—now a DOP—is grown and prized for its sweet juiciness. Grapefruit and kumquats are relatively less common, while heirloom varieties such as the sweet vanilla orange and the lumia, a very low-acid lemon, are grown in small batches for the serious citrus connoisseur.

CITRUS RISOTTO

risotto agli agrumi

SERVES 4

1 small orange

1 small lemon

1 small grapefruit

1 small onion, finely chopped

1 garlic clove, finely chopped

2 tablespoons olive oil

1½ cups (300 g) risotto rice, such as Carnaroli, Arborio, or Vialone Nano

½ cup (120 ml) dry white wine

4 to 6 cups (1 to 1.5 L) vegetable broth

4 tablespoons (55 g) unsalted butter

½ cup (50 g) finely grated Parmigiano-Reggiano cheese

Fine sea salt and freshly ground black pepper

Rice had been cultivated in the areas around Catania and Enna from the Middle Ages until relatively recently, when the swamps were drained for both public health and political reasons. Nowadays, a few Sicilian farmers are once again growing rice and producing some excellent Arborio. This recipe blends the northern technique of making risotto with Sicily's extraordinary winter citrus. A combination of zest, flesh, and juice balances the innate richness of this classic dish.

BRING A SMALL pot of water to a boil.

While the water heats up, use a vegetable peeler to remove strips of zest from all the citrus fruits, making sure to take just the thin colorful layer and avoiding any spongy white pith. Slice the zest strips into matchsticks. (Set the fruits aside.)

Add the sliced zest to the boiling water and cook until very tender, about 5 minutes. Drain well and set aside.

Meanwhile, using a very sharp knife, carefully cut away the white pith and outer membrane from the citrus to expose the flesh, following the curve of the fruit. Cut out the segments of each citrus fruit by slicing between the interior membranes and combine all the segments in a bowl. Squeeze all the juice from the pulp clinging to the remaining membranes into a separate bowl. Set the bowls aside.

In a heavy saucepan, gently sauté the onion and garlic in the olive oil over medium heat, stirring occasionally, until softened and translucent, 6 to 8 minutes. Add the rice and cook for a minute or two, stirring to coat it with the olive oil. Pour in the wine and stir to combine. Once the wine has been absorbed by the rice, add about 1 cup (240 ml) of the broth. Cook, stirring frequently, until the rice absorbs most of the broth. Continue adding ladlefuls of the broth, about 1 cup (240 ml) at a time. Each time you add broth, add a few sliced citrus zests, a couple of citrus segments, and a splash of citrus juice. (Reserve a small amount of each for garnishing the finished risotto.) When the rice is plump and tastes tender, about 20 minutes, remove the pan from the heat and add the butter and Parmigiano, vigorously shaking the pan to incorporate. Taste and season with salt and pepper.

Garnish the risotto with the remaining citrus zest, segments, and juice and serve at once.

FISH
pesce

For an island surrounded by the Mediterranean, Ionian, and Tyrrhenian Seas, Sicily does not have as much of a seafood culture as you would think. A handful of fish appear over and over in Sicilian recipes—most notably, sardines, anchovies, tuna, and swordfish—but they are often cooked in tomato sauce or other strong flavors that can obscure their delicacy. The same is true in Sardinia, the other big Italian island, where the greatest regional dish is a suckling pig known as porceddu. Why is this? Compared to dry land, the sea was always considered much more dangerous and unpredictable—it could not be counted on to provide daily food. So islanders needed to be good farmers first and foremost. Fishing was often a second choice, even for the Aeolian and Aegadian islanders, few of whom even learned to swim.

But still, there have always been intrepid fishermen along the coasts of Sicily. On warm summer nights, small fleets of fishing boats are a common sight, their lights bobbing in the distance as they search for squid and sardines. A small crowd of people may gather on the shore in the early mornings, waiting for a local fisherman to return with a few

crates of squid, mackerel, and sardines. In the past, no fish ever went to waste, as the community came up with ways to make the most of a mixed catch. Small, bony fish were excellent for making soup, while the fatty ones were saved for fillets.

The largest fishing enterprises in Sicily have been for tuna, sardines, and swordfish. In spring, schools of tuna flood into the Mediterranean Sea in search of warm waters in which to mate. The fish travel all around Sicily, surfing the north coast from Trapani to Messina early in the season before making their way along the southeast coast as they head back to the open ocean. Once upon a time, tonnare, beautiful complexes where tuna were caught and processed, dotted the entire coastline of Sicily, and this industry thrived well into the twentieth century. Sardine fishing was a staple of the small villages such as Acireale and Acitrezza on the east coast, while swordfishing mostly took place along the channel between Messina and Reggio Calabria. An amazing heritage of old swordfishing customs, tools, and even songs, dating back to the time of the Greeks, still exists around the Messina area but is in danger of disappearing because of more modern, automatized fishing boats. Before refrigeration, fishermen kept the fish fresh by storing them in huge nets called nassa, which would be stuffed with fish and left in seawater until the fish were sold at market.

Primitive roads and transport made it almost impossible to get fresh fish to the interior of Sicily. That is why dried or salted cod was so popular in this deeply Catholic country where, until the 1960s, Sicilians were expected to eat magro (meatless) every Friday and Saturday. Now, most Catholics forgo meat only on Fridays during Lent. You may still find *il pesce finto* ("the fake fish"), a sort of omelet with greens or potatoes that is shaped like a fish, or vegetarian dishes such as pasta con le sarde (see Bucatini with Sardines and Wild Fennel, page 99) served *con il pesce a mare*, which means "with the fish still in the sea." This phrase really highlights the interesting relationship Sicilians have had with food—how one can meet expectations by naming the missing ingredient and proceeding as if it were actually there.

One of the most common ways that Sicilians cook fish is alla ghiotta, made by sautéing onions and tomatoes, adding water, and then cooking the fish gently in the mixture. Once the fish is cooked, the broth can be served as is or reduced to make a thicker sauce, as in the Tuna Ragù (page 154). In Trapani, cooks often add a pesto made of almonds, parsley, and garlic to the broth. Usually, poorer fish are used for this preparation, ones that are considered rich in flavor but with more bones than flesh. In the United States, a diner would be outraged to find a bone in their fish. In Sicily, we take it for granted—just pull it out and keep eating!

SARDINES STUFFED WITH BREAD CRUMBS AND RAISINS

sarde a beccafico

SERVES 6 TO 8

1 small red onion,
very finely chopped

¼ cup (60 ml) olive oil,
plus more for drizzling

½ cup (60 g) plain dried
bread crumbs

¼ cup (35 g) raisins

¼ cup (35 g) pine nuts

¼ cup (5 g) finely chopped
fresh flat-leaf parsley

¼ cup (5 g) finely chopped
fresh mint

1½ lemons, 1 juiced,
½ thinly sliced

Fine sea salt and freshly
ground black pepper

2 pounds (900 g) very
fresh small sardines, heads
removed, cleaned and
deboned (see page 134)

½ orange, thinly sliced

12 bay leaves, preferably fresh

Sardines are ubiquitous on Sicilian menus, and this colorful dish shows up all over the island, served both as an antipasto and as a main course. The sardines are cleaned and opened *a libretto* ("like a small book") before getting rolled up with a classic Sicilian stuffing of herbed bread crumbs, pine nuts, and raisins and placed snugly in a baking dish with bay leaves and orange and lemon slices, resulting in a dish as pretty as it is tasty.

IN A SMALL skillet, cook the onion in the olive oil over medium heat until just golden, about 5 minutes. Stir in the bread crumbs and cook until toasted, about 2 minutes. Stir in the raisins, pine nuts, parsley, and mint. Remove from the heat. Add the lemon juice and salt and pepper to taste and mix well. Set the filling aside to cool.

Preheat the oven to 375°F (190°C). Lightly oil a ceramic baking dish large enough to hold all the sardines in a single layer.

Lay a sardine skin-side down, with the tail facing away from you, on a work surface. Put about 1½ teaspoons filling on the bottom third of the sardine, then roll up. Repeat with the remaining sardines and filling. Arrange the sardines snugly in the baking dish, with their tails sticking up, all in the same direction. Tuck the lemon and orange slices and bay leaves between the sardines and drizzle everything with olive oil.

Bake until tender, 15 to 20 minutes.

The sardines can be served warm or at room temperature.

NOTE: The sardines can be assembled up to 3 hours ahead and refrigerated until you are ready to bake them.

ANCHOVIES AND SARDINES

EVEN THOUGH ANCHOVIES AND SARDINES BELONG TO TWO different families, they are both oily fishes that occupy a central position in the ocean's food chain by eating plankton before becoming food themselves for bigger predators. The fish travel in huge schools, and small boats equipped with strong lights called lampare fish for them at night. Drawn to the light, the fish swim to the surface, where they are caught in nets.

Sardines and anchovies, both fresh and cured, are used extensively in Sicilian food. Most of them are cured under salt and then transferred to olive oil. However, since the oil used for preserving is rarely very good, many Sicilians prefer fish that have just been salt-cured, even though they require much more work to clean. Sardines are slightly bigger and meatier than anchovies. For pasta con le sarde (see Bucatini with Sardines and Wild Fennel, page 99) in Palermo, fresh sardines are preferable, while in Catania the same dish is made with anchovies, which are called masculini there. Sicilians are accustomed to cooking with very small, very fresh sardines, 4 to 6 inches (10 to 15 cm) in length, and the recipes in this book are written with such fish in mind. It is best to work with your local fishmonger to source them.

CLEANING FRESH SARDINES AND ANCHOVIES

There is a very specific way to clean both sardines and anchovies, which in Sicilian is called *allinguate* ("tongue wise") or *a libretto* ("like a small book"). First, pinch off the head and fins. Then use your fingertip to slit open the belly and remove the guts and spine. Holding the fish belly-up, open the body like a book. Now it is ready to be eaten raw, fried, grilled, or stuffed and baked.

MACKEREL DUMPLINGS IN TOMATO SAUCE

polpettine di sgombro al sugo

SERVES 4

FOR THE MACKEREL DUMPLINGS

9 ounces (250 g) fresh mackerel fillets, cut into 1-inch (2.5 cm) chunks

2 tablespoons finely chopped wild fennel fronds (optional)

1 tablespoon finely chopped fresh flat-leaf parsley, plus more for serving

Finely grated zest of ½ orange

1 tablespoon pistachios

½ teaspoon ground cumin

½ teaspoon ground coriander

½ teaspoon paprika

½ cup (60 g) plain dried bread crumbs

1 large egg

½ teaspoon fine sea salt

¼ teaspoon freshly ground black pepper

FOR THE SAUCE

½ medium yellow onion, finely chopped

3 tablespoons olive oil

Pinch of ground cinnamon

Pinch of saffron, soaked in ¼ cup (60 ml) white wine

Pinch of fennel seeds

1 bay leaf

3 cups (720 ml) good-quality tomato sauce, homemade (page 87) or store-bought

Mackerel season in Sicily falls between March and June, when the fish venture close to shore to spawn, ideally making their way into the fisherman's net after they have released their eggs. Mackerel, a so-called "fatty fish" and a close relative of tuna, has firm and flavorful meat. These tomato-braised "meatballs," seasoned with plenty of fresh herbs and spices, are a way to appeal to non–fish lovers. Fortunately, they are very delicious in their own right! Though you could serve them with pasta, the polpettine are good with just some crusty bread and a salad or cooked greens. If you can't find mackerel, another firm, white-fleshed fish such as cod or monkfish can be used.

MAKE THE MACKEREL dumplings: In a food processor, combine the mackerel, wild fennel (if using), parsley, orange zest, pistachios, cumin, coriander, paprika, bread crumbs, egg, salt, and pepper and blend until the mixture comes together and everything is well incorporated. (Alternatively, you can very finely chop the fish by hand and then mix it with the other ingredients.)

Use your hands to shape the fish mixture into 2-inch (5 cm) balls and set them aside while you make the sauce.

Make the sauce: In a large saucepan wide enough to hold the dumplings in a single layer, sauté the onion in the olive oil over medium heat until golden, about 5 minutes. Add the cinnamon, saffron (with its soaking liquid), fennel seeds, and bay leaf. Cook, stirring, for 1 to 2 minutes. Pour in the tomato sauce and bring to a boil. Reduce the heat and simmer until slightly thickened, 5 to 10 minutes.

Add the fish dumplings in a single layer to the sauce. Cover the pan and cook, turning the dumplings occasionally, until cooked through, 12 to 15 minutes.

Sprinkle with fresh flat-leaf parsley and serve warm or at room temperature.

NOTE: The fish dumplings can be shaped up to 3 hours ahead and refrigerated. The sauce can be made up to 2 days ahead and refrigerated. Gently reheat the sauce, adding a splash of water if necessary to thin it, before adding and cooking the dumplings.

MACKEREL CONFIT

confit di sgombro

SERVES 4

1½ pounds (680 g) fresh
mackerel fillets, about 1 inch
(2.5 cm) thick

Fine sea salt and freshly
ground black pepper

4 cups (1 L) olive oil, plus
more as needed

2 lemons

3 sprigs fresh thyme

3 sprigs fresh mint leaves

EQUIPMENT
Instant-read thermometer

Chef Corrado Assenza, who owns Caffè Sicilia in Noto, likes to poach mackerel fillets very gently in warm olive oil, a different approach than what is used in so many other classic Sicilian recipes. The fish remains incredibly moist, and the flavor is exceptional. The recipe calls for a large amount of olive oil, which will taste a bit fishy after you're done, but it can be strained and reused to fry or poach another kind of fish.

PLACE THE MACKEREL fillets on a plate and let rest at room temperature for 1 hour. Right before poaching, sprinkle lightly with salt and pepper and rub the spices into the fish.

Pour 4 cups (1 L) of the olive oil into a sauté pan large enough to hold all the fillets in a single layer. Using a vegetable peeler, remove wide strips of zest from one of the lemons and add it to the pan along with the thyme and mint. Using an instant-read thermometer to monitor the temperature, heat the olive oil over medium-low heat until it reaches 122°F (50°C). As soon as the oil is the correct temperature, carefully slide the fillets into the pan. There should be enough oil to cover the fish by ¼ inch (6 mm); if there isn't, add a little more oil to the pan. Immediately turn off the heat, cover the pan, and let the fish cook in the hot oil until firm, 20 to 25 minutes.

Gently lift the fillets out of the oil and place them on a serving platter. Sprinkle lightly with salt and pepper.

Cut the remaining lemon into slices and place them on the platter to serve with the fish.

FISH MARKETS

THE FISH MARKETS ON THE EAST COAST OF SICILY ARE QUITE spectacular—vibrant and colorful, with crates, tables, and buckets loaded with fish, and aproned men shouting to one another and vying for customers' attention. Indeed, a fish market is always a fascinating place to study Sicilian gestures and faces! Today, Catania has the biggest and most well-known fish market, but the smaller markets in Siracusa and Trapani are also well worth exploring.

It can be difficult for cooks in certain areas to find the kinds of fish and cuts that Sicilians take for granted, whether it is small, bony fish for making stock for Fish Soup with Steamed Couscous (page 72) or large cross-sections of swordfish or tuna called for in Swordfish Stuffed with Garlic and Mint (page 149) or Tuna Ragù (page 154). When making stock, look for rockfish, scorpion fish, sand dab, and other small fish with white meat, as well as the heads of big fish such as cod, halibut, and sea bass; avoid oily fish such as tuna, bonito, yellowfin, salmon, et cetera.

In Sicilian fish markets during tuna or swordfish season, you will often see whole giant fish on ice waiting to be butchered, which makes it easy for the fishmonger to simply cut off whatever piece you need. Outside of Sicily, supermarkets tend to focus on selling already boned-out portions of a limited selection of large fish, such as tuna, swordfish, salmon, and cod. However, Asian markets and specialty fish markets, especially in big coastal cities, usually offer a greater variety of fresh fish on a regular basis. Wherever you are, it's worth developing a relationship with a local fishmonger so they can help you get what you want; calling ahead to preorder always helps, too.

GRILLED SQUID WITH SALMORIGLIO SAUCE

calamari alla griglia con salmoriglio

SERVES 6

1 garlic clove, coarsely chopped

1 tablespoon dried oregano, preferably wild (see Resources, page 310)

¾ cup (180 ml) olive oil

6 tablespoons (90 ml) fresh lemon juice

¾ teaspoon fine sea salt

2 pounds (900 g) cleaned squid bodies and tentacles

The word *salmoriglio* comes from *salamoia*, meaning "brine." This lemony, oily sauce, a specialty of Sicily and other parts of Southern Italy, makes good use of dried oregano, which grows wild all over the Mediterranean, and it's worth seeking out the best you can find (see Resources, page 310). Salmoriglio is delicious spooned over any type of fish or meat that can handle the high heat of a grill or grill pan, from squid and swordfish steaks to lamb chops.

IN A SMALL bowl, whisk together the garlic, oregano, olive oil, lemon juice, and salt until the salt has dissolved. Taste the salmoriglio sauce and adjust the seasonings.

Heat a grill or grill pan to high. Carefully place the squid on the hot grill. Grill, turning occasionally, until lightly charred all over, about 5 minutes. Remove from the grill. If you like, cut the squid into smaller pieces or serve whole.

Serve the squid drizzled with some of the salmoriglio sauce, serving the rest on the side.

NOTE: Leftover salmoriglio sauce will keep for up to 2 weeks in the refrigerator.

BREADED SWORDFISH

pesce spada impanato

SERVES 6

One 2¼-pound (1 kg) piece of swordfish, cut into steaks ¼ inch (6 mm) thick

¼ cup (60 ml) olive oil, plus more for panfrying

1 teaspoon fine sea salt

2 tablespoons dried oregano, preferably wild (see Resources, page 310)

¼ cup (5 g) chopped fresh flat-leaf parsley leaves

¼ cup (5 g) chopped fresh mint leaves

2 garlic cloves, sliced

Pinch of crushed red pepper flakes

1½ cups (190 g) plain dried bread crumbs

Lemon wedges, for serving

A classic of Palermitan cuisine, this straightforward dish—swordfish steaks that have been marinated and coated in bread crumbs—is a real crowd-pleaser. We give instructions for panfrying, but the fish can be cooked as you please: on the stove, in the oven, or even on a grill. In any case, the cooking will be fast—you want a good toasty crunch from the bread crumbs. Don't worry if some of the steaks char slightly; it's all part of the rough-and-ready appeal of this dish, which goes well with roasted potatoes or something fresh like Tomato and Purslane Salad (page 197). Ask your fishmonger to slice the steaks for you.

PLACE THE SWORDFISH in a dish, drizzle the olive oil evenly over it, and season with the salt. Sprinkle the oregano, parsley, mint, garlic, and pepper flakes evenly over both sides of the fish. Cover and marinate in the refrigerator for 1 to 2 hours.

Spread the bread crumbs in a shallow dish. Working with one piece of marinated swordfish at a time, press each side into the bread crumbs, coating the fish evenly.

Heat a large skillet over medium-high heat. Pour enough olive oil into the pan to lightly coat the bottom. Place as many pieces of fish as will fit comfortably without crowding in the pan and cook until golden brown on the first side, 2 to 3 minutes. Flip and cook on the other side until just barely cooked through and opaque in the center, about 2 minutes more. Transfer to a platter. Repeat to panfry the other breaded fish pieces.

Serve at once, with lemon wedges on the side.

SWORDFISH STUFFED WITH GARLIC AND MINT

ruota di pesce spada in padella

SERVES 10 TO 12

FOR THE FISH

¼ cup (60 ml) olive oil, plus more for the roasting pan

4½ pounds (2 kg) swordfish or tuna, cut in one thick cross section

2 garlic cloves, peeled

¼ cup (5 g) fresh mint leaves

Fine sea salt and freshly ground black pepper

1 red onion, coarsely chopped

½ cup (120 ml) white wine

FOR THE SAUCE

4 to 6 tablespoons (60 to 90 ml) red or white wine vinegar

¼ cup (60 ml) fresh lemon juice

1 teaspoon sugar

½ cup (120 ml) olive oil

2 garlic cloves, minced

2 tablespoons salt-packed capers, rinsed and coarsely chopped

2 tablespoons chopped fresh oregano

2 tablespoons chopped fresh flat-leaf parsley leaves

2 tablespoons chopped fresh mint leaves

2 tablespoons chopped fresh thyme

Fine sea salt and freshly ground black pepper

EQUIPMENT

Instant-read thermometer (optional)

Roasting a really large piece of fish as you would a piece of red meat makes for an impressive dish that stays juicy through and through. You will most likely need to special-order the fish from your local fishmonger, but otherwise the preparation could not be easier. A fresh, tangy sauce full of green herbs and capers adds the final touch and would be equally delicious served over any type of grilled or roasted meat.

ROAST THE FISH: Preheat the oven to 375°F (190°C). Lightly oil a roasting pan large enough to comfortably fit the fish.

Using a small sharp knife, cut slits 1 inch (2.5 cm) deep all over the fish. Place the garlic and mint on a cutting board and chop together until very finely chopped and well combined. Push the mixture into the slits, rubbing any leftover bits over the outside. Season the fish all over with salt and pepper. Place the fish in the prepared roasting pan, scatter the onion evenly on top, and drizzle with the ¼ cup (60 ml) olive oil.

Roast for 10 minutes, then pour the wine over the fish. Continue to roast until the fish is cooked through and opaque in the middle, about 15 minutes. Test for doneness by inserting the tip of a small knife into the thickest part of the fish and holding it to your lip; when the fish is done, the knife should slide in easily and be warm when held to your lip. (Alternatively, use a meat thermometer to test the temperature of the fish, taking the fish out of the oven when it reaches 135° to 140°F/57° to 60°C.)

While the fish is roasting, make the sauce: In a medium bowl, stir together the vinegar, lemon juice, and sugar until the sugar has dissolved. Whisk in the olive oil, garlic, capers, and herbs. Season to taste with salt and pepper. Set aside.

When the fish is done, transfer it to a serving platter and spoon the pan juices over it. Give the sauce a stir, then spoon some over the fish. Serve the rest of the sauce on the side.

DOUBLE-CRUST SWORDFISH PIE

impanata di pesce spada

-photo page 126-

-photo page 126-

SERVES 8

FOR THE DOUGH

4¾ cups (570 g) all-purpose flour

¾ cup (180 g) lard, plus more for greasing the pan

¼ cup (50 g) sugar

Finely grated zest of 1 orange

¼ cup (60 ml) white wine

1 large egg

1 large egg yolk

Pinch of fine sea salt

¼ cup (60 ml) water, or as needed

FOR THE FILLING

1 medium onion, diced

3 small celery stalks, diced

8 tablespoons (120 ml) olive oil

3 tablespoons estratto (sun-dried tomato paste; see Resources, page 310) or other good-quality tomato paste

½ cup (120 ml) white wine

½ cup (100 g) black olives, pitted and finely chopped

⅓ cup (50 g) salt-packed capers, rinsed and coarsely chopped

Swordfish and tuna are the two "aristocratic" fishes of Sicily and, not surprisingly, they became the stars of imposing dishes like the Swordfish Stuffed with Garlic and Mint (page 149) and this impanata, a rich, slightly sweet pastry filled with chunks of fish, olives, capers, and fried rounds of zucchini. Originally from the coastal city of Messina, where swordfishing was treated as an art, this is an elaborate recipe, yes, but one that satisfies on a very deep level. Consider serving this with a big green salad, sautéed greens, or the Green Beans with Anchovies and Bread Crumbs (page 211).

MAKE THE DOUGH: In a large bowl, combine the flour, lard, sugar, orange zest, wine, whole egg, egg yolk, and salt. Mix until the dough comes together into a ball, adding a little water only if you need it to help the dough come together. Divide the dough into 2 pieces, one slightly larger than the other, and flatten into discs. Wrap each in plastic wrap and refrigerate for about 2 hours.

Make the filling: In a large skillet, sauté the onion and celery in 3 tablespoons of the olive oil over medium heat until the onion softens, about 5 minutes. Dissolve the estratto in the wine, then add the mixture to the pan, along with the olives and capers. Season lightly with salt and pepper. (The olives and capers are quite salty already.) Add the swordfish and cook, stirring occasionally, until the fish begins to turn opaque, about 3 minutes (it will finish cooking in the oven). Remove from the heat and let cool.

Meanwhile, set a wire rack in a sheet pan. In a separate skillet, heat the remaining 5 tablespoons olive oil over medium heat. Working in batches if necessary, cook the zucchini slices, turning once, until softened and golden, about 5 minutes. Transfer the zucchini to the rack to drain.

Once the dough has chilled, preheat the oven to 350°F (180°C). Generously grease a 10-inch (25 cm) springform pan.

Roll out each piece of dough into a round about ¼ inch (6 mm) thick. Drape the larger round across the prepared pan as the

Fine sea salt and freshly ground black pepper

1 pound 5 ounces (600 g) swordfish steaks, cut into 1-inch (2.5 cm) cubes

1 pound 5 ounces (600 g) zucchini, cut into slices ¼ inch (6 mm) thick

EQUIPMENT
10-inch (25 cm) springform pan

bottom crust, pressing the dough into the bottom and up the sides of the pan. Arrange half of the zucchini slices evenly along the bottom of the pastry, then spoon in the swordfish filling. Cover with an even layer of the remaining zucchini. Cover the pie with the smaller dough round and use your fingers to crimp all the way around the edge, sealing the top and bottom crusts. Prick the top of the pastry with a fork in several places for venting.

Bake until the pastry is golden brown, 40 to 45 minutes. Let cool for 20 minutes on a wire rack before unmolding the pie from the pan.

Serve warm or at room temperature.

NOTE: The dough can be made up to 1 day ahead and refrigerated.

MONSÙ CUISINE

AFTER THE FRENCH REVOLUTION, FRENCH CUISINE BECAME THE gold standard for the ruling class everywhere in Europe. This trend reached Sicily in the beginning of the 1800s, when Ferdinand I of the Two Sicilies (the merged kingdoms of Sicily and Naples), whose wife was a sister of Marie Antoinette's, had to flee the revolution and escaped (twice!) from Naples to Palermo. His second stay lasted eight years, long enough to have a lasting influence on Sicilian food.

The arrival of French techniques to Sicily, where food was already quite complex, formed a very particular way of cooking—half Sicilian, half French—that became known as monsù cuisine (*monsù* being a corruption of the French *monsieur*). What came out of this time, when the aristocracy led the world and Palermo's numerous palazzos were teeming with parties and balls, was a series of superbly decorated dishes, seasoned with butter, cream, prosciutto, and even truffles, none of which were native to Sicily. Deep-fried béchamel and pâte à choux, gratinéed wild greens laden with butter, cinnamon-scented brioche with ice cream—these are just some of the delicious concoctions that came out of this period.

Today, few families in Sicily still make this kind of food, but the influence of monsù cuisine remains, in some surprising places. You can find it most clearly in the local rosticceria (see page 233), where "stand-up food," such as fluffy calzones and brioche stuffed with gelato, are everyday treats.

TUNA RAGÙ

tonno ammuttunatu

SERVES 6 TO 8

4½-pound (2 kg) piece tuna

6 garlic cloves, finely chopped

½ cup (10 g) fresh mint, finely chopped

1¾ ounces (50 g) caciocavallo cheese, finely chopped or grated

4 large onions, thinly sliced

½ cup (120 ml) olive oil

1 cup (240 ml) white wine

2 tablespoons estratto (sun-dried tomato paste; see Resources, page 310) or other good-quality tomato paste

3 cups (720 ml) boiling water

2 cups (480 ml) good-quality tomato sauce, homemade (page 87) or store-bought, plus more as needed

Tuna ragù is a celebratory dish that requires one large piece of fish and takes some time to cook. The rich tomato sauce that is created is meant to be served with pasta as a primo piatto; the tuna itself should be the main, but of course you can choose to serve everything all at once. Talk to a fishmonger who can provide a big chunk of tuna, ideally bluefin or albacore (yellowfin is too lean for this preparation). If possible, ask them to cut a piece from the lower belly—the fattiest part of the tuna—so the tuna stays moist while it cooks.

USING A SMALL sharp knife, cut slits 1 inch (2.5 cm) deep all over the tuna. In a small bowl, stir together the chopped garlic, mint, and caciocavallo. Press the mixture into the slits, rubbing any excess over the surface of the fish.

In a large heavy-bottomed saucepan, cook the onions in the olive oil over medium heat, stirring occasionally, until pale golden, about 5 minutes. Drizzle in ½ cup (120 ml) of the white wine and cook, stirring occasionally, until the wine has evaporated, about 5 minutes. Scrape the onions into a bowl and set aside.

Place the tuna in the pan, drizzle with the remaining ½ cup (120 ml) wine, and cook over medium heat until lightly browned on each side, 5 to 8 minutes. Transfer the tuna to a plate.

Dissolve the estratto in the boiling water and add to the empty pan, along with the tomato sauce and the sautéed onions. Bring to a boil, then add the tuna; the fish should be almost submerged in the sauce. Return to a boil, then lower the heat to medium-low, partially cover, and cook gently until the sauce has thickened and the tuna is fully cooked, 2½ to 3 hours (check the tuna's doneness by sticking a sharp narrow knife into the meat; it should slide in easily). Flip the tuna a few times during cooking. The sauce will reduce but should always stay at least halfway up the tuna. If the sauce is too liquidy once the tuna has fully cooked, remove the fish from the pan and simmer the sauce alone until it reaches the desired consistency.

If desired, serve the sauce alone with cooked pasta as a first course, and then the tuna as a main course. Or serve everything all together.

NOTE: Any leftover sauce can be refrigerated for up to 3 days or frozen for up to 1 month.

SALT COD SALAD

insalata di baccalà

SERVES 6

2 pounds (900 g) salt cod

1 cup (150 g) cherry tomatoes, halved

2 celery stalks, thinly sliced

½ small red onion, sliced

½ cup (90 g) black olives, pitted and halved

¼ cup (30 g) salt-packed capers, rinsed

½ cup (120 ml) olive oil

1 teaspoon dried oregano, preferably wild (see Resources, page 310)

Fine sea salt and freshly ground black pepper

This salad is typical of the area around Messina, where it may be made with either baccalà (salted cod) or stoccafisso (dried cod). Outside of Sicily, baccalà is often easier to find than stoccafisso; it also has the benefit of being meatier. Most Sicilians have a relationship with a local fishmonger who will soak the fish for them, which makes this colorful salad quick to pull together.

RINSE THE EXCESS salt off the salt cod. Submerge the fish in a bowl of cold water and refrigerate for 24 hours, changing the water three times. At the end of the soaking time, the fish should feel almost fresh again and taste just pleasantly salted.

Drain the salt cod and put it in a large pot. Add cold water to cover. Bring to a boil, then reduce the heat to medium-low and simmer until the fish is tender, about 15 minutes. Drain.

When the fish is cool enough to handle, remove any bones, fins, and tough pieces of skin. Break the fish into 1-inch (2.5 cm) chunks and transfer to a bowl.

Add the tomatoes, celery, red onion, olives, capers, olive oil, and oregano. Toss gently to combine. Season to taste with salt and pepper.

NOTE: The salad can be made up to 1 day ahead and refrigerated.

MEAT
carne

ROAST CHICKEN WITH ORANGES 162
pollo all'arancia

**BRAISED RABBIT WITH
BLACK OLIVES AND ROSEMARY 167**
coniglio alle olive nere e rosmarino

**STEWED LAMB WITH FRESH MINT
AND SAFFRON POTATOES 168**
spezzatino di agnello alla menta e
patate allo zafferano

LAMB-STUFFED PASTRY 169
impanata di agnello

**ROAST PORK WITH MINT AND
GARLIC 175**
arista di maiale

**GRILLED SAUSAGE WITH
BAY LEAVES AND ONIONS 178**
salsiccia con alloro e cipolla

MEAT ROLL-UPS 179
involtini di carne

SICILIAN MEATLOAF 184
polpettone

As soon as there are holidays to celebrate, such as Pasquetta (the day after Easter) or Ferragosto (a traditional day of rest for agricultural workers, celebrated on August 15), Sicilians get ready to barbecue. The entire day will be given over to cooking and eating with family and friends, and this joyful gathering can happen almost anywhere—at the beach, in a park, up in the mountains, or even on a street corner in the town center. There are no set rules. But wherever people choose to gather, the grill will be at the center of it all, as a steady progression of vegetables and meats— bony lamb chops, coils of fennel-flecked sausages, spring onions wrapped in pancetta (amusingly called *mangia e bevi*, or "eat and drink"), even stigghiole (lamb's intestines wrapped around a mixture of onion and parsley)—take their turn over the coals. The aroma of roasting meat can follow your car for miles outside of the city.

Barbecues aside, Sicilians have never been big meat eaters, mostly due to scarcity. According to historians, meat disappeared from the everyday table after the sixteenth century, when intensive farming killed off much of the island's wild animal population. Only the very privileged—nobles and religious leaders—could afford to eat meat regularly. Everyone else made do with cheese, bread, legumes, and vegetables, a trend that continued into the twentieth century. Most Sicilian farmers would keep a few chickens and go hunting, mainly for hares and various game birds. For those living in the mountains, where the climate allows for the longer preservation of raw meat, pork was essential to the peasant diet, being one of the few sources of protein that people in small villages could afford. The family pig would get butchered during winter, and every single part would be eaten fresh or tucked away for the coming months. If a family was fortunate enough to own cows, they were mainly for work and for milk.

Older generations were much more familiar with wild, gamy flavors, and the idea of eating mutton or meat from the Razza Modicana cow or suino nero, the black pig that forages in the forest undergrowth of the Nebrodi Mountains, was common. Younger people are no longer accustomed to those strong flavors, and meat in many Sicilian households is often very simple: chicken breast and lean cutlets. Lamb is still a staple at Easter, but it needs to be young and mild.

Perhaps in reaction to the centuries of deprivation, every village now has several butcher shops called *carnezzerie*, a word used only in Sicily (the rest of Italy calls them *macellerie*). In rural villages, butchers generally offer a limited range of cuts from locally raised animals, with the most popular items being things like sliced cutlets for involtini or impanato, chicken breasts, ground meat, and sausage. But the carnezzeria is not just a place to buy meat; it is a gathering place, especially in small towns. Behind the click-clacking plastic beaded curtain that keeps the flies out, there are always a few chairs where retired men or the butcher's family can sit and chat with one another and the customers.

ROAST CHICKEN WITH ORANGES

pollo all'arancia

SERVES 6

Olive oil, for the pan

1 whole chicken
(about 4 pounds/1.8 kg)

1 yellow onion, peeled
and quartered

1 lemon, quartered

2 large sprigs fresh rosemary

2 tablespoons mixed
dried herbs

1 teaspoon fine sea salt

½ teaspoon freshly ground
black pepper

¾ cup (180 ml) fresh orange
juice, preferably from blood
oranges

¾ cup (180 ml) white wine

EQUIPMENT
Instant-read thermometer
(optional)

Herbs grow easily and abundantly under Sicily's hot sun, and home cooks often dry their own and make blends that can be used all year long. For this roast chicken, a combination of dried rosemary, sage, bay leaf, mint, geranium, chile, and orange peel works beautifully against the acidity of the wine and citrus. If possible, seek out blood oranges such as Sanguinello, Tarocco, or Moro, which have more complexity than the straight-ahead sweetness of navel oranges.

PREHEAT THE OVEN to 400°F (200°C). Oil a roasting pan big enough to hold the chicken.

Stuff the chicken with the onion quarters, lemon quarters, and rosemary sprigs. Sprinkle the dried herbs, salt, and pepper evenly over the chicken, top and bottom, and gently massage into the skin.

Place the chicken in the pan and roast for about 50 minutes, then pour the orange juice and wine over the chicken. Continue roasting until the skin is crisp and nicely browned, the meat's juices run clear, and the pan juices are reduced and syrupy, 10 to 15 minutes more. If using a meat thermometer, the thickest part of the thigh should register 165°F (75°C).

Remove the chicken from the oven and let rest for at least 10 minutes before carving it. Serve it with its pan juices.

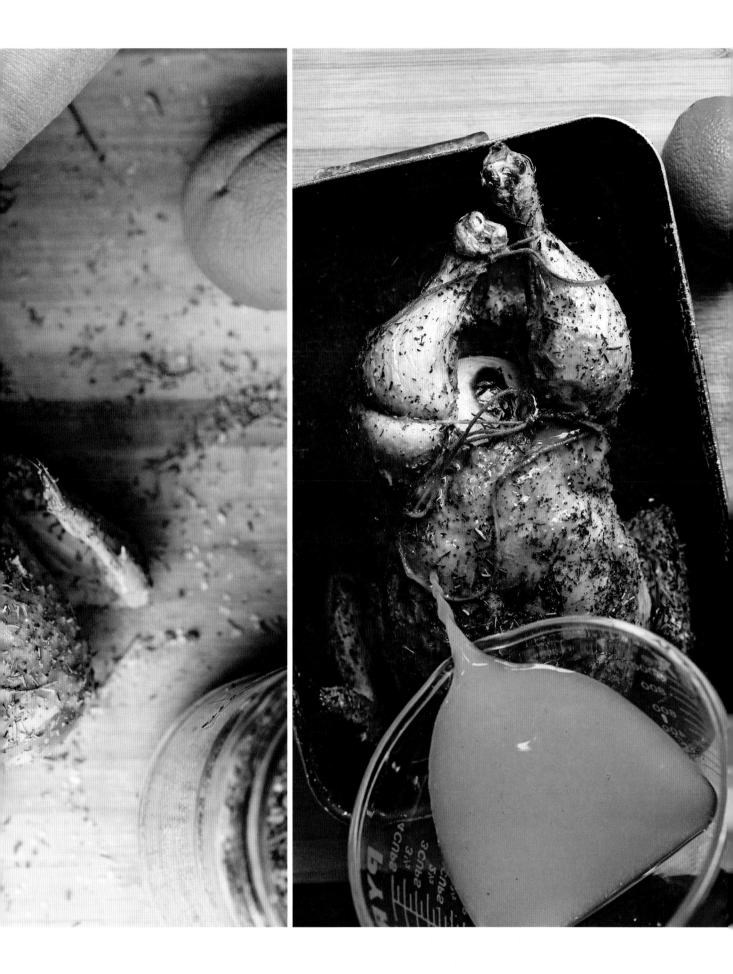

BRAISED RABBIT WITH BLACK OLIVES AND ROSEMARY

coniglio alle olive nere e rosmarino

SERVES 6

1 yellow onion, sliced

2 celery stalks, sliced

½ cup (120 ml) olive oil

1 whole rabbit (about 3½ pounds/1.5 kg), cut into 8 pieces

Fine sea salt and freshly ground black pepper

1 tablespoon estratto (sun-dried tomato paste; see Resources, page 310) or other good-quality tomato paste

1 cup (240 ml) white wine

5 sprigs fresh rosemary

5 sprigs fresh sage

1 to 2 cups (240 to 480 ml) water

2 cups (270 g) black olives, pitted

Until a few decades ago, any man living in rural Sicily would consider himself a hunter, and wild hare was one of the most cherished game options available. But farming and extinction have drastically reduced the island's wildlife. Hare has become so rare that rabbit, which may be ordered from the local butcher shop, is more frequently found on Sicilian tables. Braising it with plenty of plump black olives and rosemary creates a rich sauce that helps balance the leanness of the meat. This same preparation can be made with chicken pieces. Consider serving this with Borage Risotto (page 120) or Spinach Flan (page 223).

IN A LARGE sauté pan with a lid, sauté the onion and celery in the olive oil over medium heat, stirring occasionally, until golden, 5 to 7 minutes. Season the rabbit all over with salt and pepper, then add it to the pan and cook, turning once, until nicely browned all over, about 10 minutes.

Dissolve the estratto in the wine, then pour the mixture into the pan and cook, stirring frequently, until it evaporates. Add the rosemary and sage. Pour in just enough water to nearly cover the meat. Bring to a boil, then reduce the heat to a simmer, cover, and cook until the rabbit is cooked through and tender, about 1 hour.

Uncover the pan, add the olives, and cook over medium-high heat until the sauce thickens slightly, about 5 minutes. Taste and season with salt and pepper. Serve warm.

NOTE: The braised rabbit can be made up to 1 day ahead, cooled completely, and refrigerated. Reheat gently over medium heat, covered, until heated through.

STEWED LAMB WITH FRESH MINT AND SAFFRON POTATOES

spezzatino di agnello alla menta e patate allo zafferano

SERVES 6 TO 8

1 large red onion, chopped

½ cup (120 ml) olive oil

3½ pounds (1.5 kg) boneless lamb shoulder or leg, cut into 2-inch (5 cm) pieces

Fine sea salt and freshly ground black pepper

1 tablespoon estratto (sun-dried tomato paste; see Resources, page 310) or other good-quality tomato paste

1 cup (240 ml) white wine

1 teaspoon saffron threads

6 cups (1.4 L) water

1½ pounds (680 g) small potatoes, peeled and quartered

Leaves from 1 large bunch of fresh mint, chopped

In decades past, this flavorful *spezzatino*—the Italian word for "stewed meat"—would have been made with mutton and simmered for hours to tame its gamy toughness. Today, tender, mild lamb is more often used. Potatoes are added toward the end of cooking, releasing their starches and thickening the stew.

IN A LARGE heavy pot, cook the onion in the olive oil over medium-high heat, stirring occasionally, until just golden, about 5 minutes. Season the lamb all over with salt and pepper, add to the pot, and stir until well coated in oil.

In a small bowl, stir the estratto into the wine until dissolved, then pour the mixture into the pot and cook until the liquid evaporates, about 5 minutes.

In a large measuring cup, combine the saffron and water. Pour the saffron liquid over the lamb, cover the pot, and bring to a boil. Lower the heat and simmer, covered, until the lamb is fork-tender, 45 minutes to 1 hour.

Add the potatoes to the pot and continue to cook, uncovered, until the meat and potatoes are tender and the sauce has thickened somewhat, about 20 minutes.

Add the mint, season to taste with salt and pepper, and serve.

NOTE: The stew can be made up to the point of adding the mint up to 3 days ahead and refrigerated. Reheat gently until hot and add the mint, salt, and pepper just before serving.

LAMB-STUFFED PASTRY

impanata di agnello

SERVES 6

FOR THE DOUGH

¾ teaspoon active dry yeast

1 teaspoon honey

8 tablespoons (120 ml) lukewarm water

1½ cups (240 g) semolina flour

½ teaspoon fine sea salt

3 tablespoons olive oil

FOR THE FILLING

1½ pounds (680 g) boneless leg of lamb or shoulder, cut into 1-inch (2.5 cm) cubes

Fine sea salt and freshly ground black pepper

2 tablespoons olive oil

1 small onion, chopped

1 carrot, chopped

1 celery stalk, chopped

2 garlic cloves, minced

2 teaspoons estratto (sun-dried tomato paste; see Resources, page 310) or other good-quality tomato paste

½ cup (120 ml) white wine

2 tablespoons finely chopped fresh flat-leaf parsley

2 tablespoons finely chopped fresh mint

1 large egg, lightly beaten

2 teaspoons sesame seeds

Lamb is enjoyed all over Sicily in many ways, from grilled chops to simmered stews. This pastry, an Easter staple in Ragusa, is unique on the island. The word *impanata* comes from the Spanish *empanada*, one of the many holdovers from two centuries of Spanish domination on this side of Sicily. Serve this hearty pie with Stuffed Artichokes (page 208) or Honey-Roasted Fennel and Cardoons (page 205).

MAKE THE DOUGH: In a small bowl, dissolve the yeast and honey in 2 tablespoons of the warm water. Let sit until creamy, about 5 minutes. If the mixture does not foam, start over with fresh yeast.

In a large bowl, combine the semolina, salt, olive oil, and the dissolved yeast mixture and mix well. Gradually stir in the remaining 6 tablespoons (90 ml) water—you might not need to add it all—until the dough just comes together. Transfer the dough to a clean work surface and knead it into a firm ball. Let it rest for 10 minutes, then knead it again until the dough has an even, velvety surface.

Divide the dough into 2 pieces, one slightly larger than the other. Shape each piece into a smooth ball, cover with a kitchen towel, and let rest until almost doubled in size, about 1 hour.

Meanwhile, make the filling: Place the lamb in a large bowl and season all over with salt and plenty of pepper. Set aside.

In a large sauté pan, combine the olive oil, onion, carrot, celery, and garlic. Cook over medium heat, stirring, until the vegetables start to soften, about 5 minutes. Stir in the seasoned lamb and cook until the meat starts to take on some color, about 5 minutes. Dissolve the estratto in the wine and add the mixture to the pan. Cook, stirring occasionally, until the lamb is almost cooked through and the liquid evaporates, about 10 minutes. Remove the pan from the heat and stir in the parsley and mint. Let cool.

When the dough has almost finished rising, preheat the oven to 300°F (150°C). Line a baking sheet with parchment paper.

Roll out the larger ball of dough into an 11-inch (28 cm) round and place on the prepared baking sheet. Roll the smaller ball of dough into a 9-inch (23 cm) round. Mound the lamb mixture in the middle of the larger round, then drape the smaller round over it and pinch the edges together to seal in the filling. Cut 2 or 3 small holes in the dough for steam to escape. Brush the pastry with the egg and sprinkle with the sesame seeds.

Bake until golden brown, about 40 minutes. Remove from the oven and cover with a clean kitchen towel. Let rest for at least 20 minutes before cutting into wedges and serving.

MOUNTAINS

ITALY'S BACKBONE IS THE APENNINES—A LONG MOUNTAIN chain that runs lengthwise down the whole country. A tip of that chain reaches into northern Sicily and produces other major mountainous blocks that traverse the island from east to west. Driving from the balmy coast into the Nebrodi Mountains, starting near Messina and moving west toward Palermo, is like entering a different country: The steep mountains, shrouded in mist and patchworked with olive groves and forest, slide abruptly into the Tyrrhenian Sea. Narrow, bumpy roads with spectacular views lead you to some of Sicily's oldest fortified towns, built by the Norman warriors who arrived during the Middle Ages and started their conquest from this area.

These mountains are one of the few places left in which the beech and oak forests that once covered all of Sicily remain, and that is most likely why semiwild animals such as the suino nero thrive here. This indigenous black pig, an agile animal with long legs, has adapted well to its rough life in the mountains, running in packs and feeding on fallen acorns.

Continuing through the Nebrodi and on to the Madonie Mountains reveals spiky peaks alternating with vast plateaus that range from bright green in winter and spring to straw gold in summer and fall. All year long, herds of cows graze on the grass while flocks of sheep dot the hills, watched over by vigilant shepherds. Not surprisingly, both mountain regions are known for their cheeses: Pecorino, made from sheep's milk, and provola, made from cow's milk (see Sicilian Cheeses, page 114).

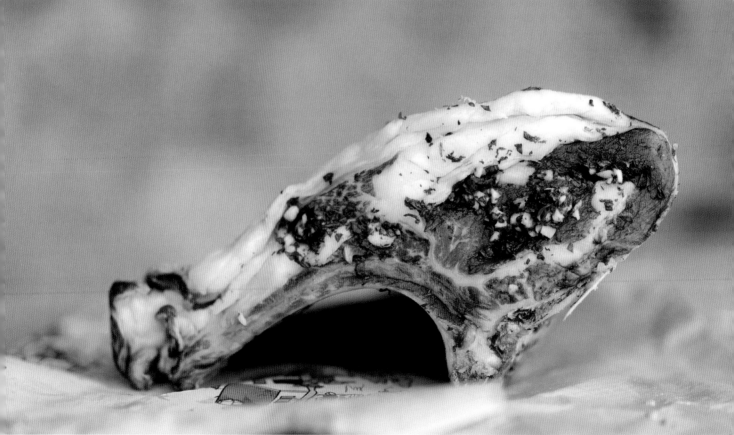

ROAST PORK WITH MINT AND GARLIC

arista di maiale

SERVES 8

Olive oil, for the pan

1 bone-in pork loin roast
(about 3⅓ pounds/1.5 kg)

½ cup (10 g) finely chopped
fresh mint

4 garlic cloves, minced

1 teaspoon fine sea salt

1 cup (240 ml) white wine

EQUIPMENT
Instant-read thermometer

The meat from the suino nero, or black pig of the Nebrodi Mountains, would traditionally be used for this impressive roast, so seek out the best pasture-raised pork you can find. The quality should be apparent in the thick layer of snow-white lardo, or fat, attached to the meat. Ask your butcher to keep the meat on the bone, which preserves its moistness and enhances its flavor. The bright flavors of fresh mint and garlic are a natural partner to the rich, deeply flavored pork.

PREHEAT THE OVEN to 400°F (200°C). Drizzle a medium roasting pan with olive oil.

Place the pork roast in the roasting pan. Using a small, sharp knife, cut slits 1 inch (2.5 cm) deep all over the meat. In a small bowl, stir together the mint, garlic, and salt. Press the herb mixture into the slits, rubbing any excess over the surface of the meat.

Roast the pork for 30 minutes. Drizzle the wine over the meat and continue roasting until the pork is crisp and browned on the outside and a thermometer inserted in the center of the roast registers 135°F (57°C), about 1 hour more.

Remove from the oven, cover loosely with foil, and let rest for 20 minutes (as the pork rests, the temperature should rise to 145°F/63°C).

Slice the pork roast between the bones into chops and serve with the pan juices collected in the baking dish.

NOTE: Leftovers can be stored in an airtight container in the fridge for up to 3 days.

GRILLED SAUSAGE WITH BAY LEAVES AND ONIONS

salsiccia con alloro e cipolla

-photo page 158-

SERVES 4 TO 6

2¼ pounds (1 kg) coiled fresh Italian sausage

1 small red onion, cut into sixths

6 to 8 fresh bay leaves

EQUIPMENT

12-inch (30 cm) metal or wooden skewers

You'll find this classic dish at any Sicilian cookout, though its ease makes it a perfect choice for weeknight cooking, too. It's beautiful to look at and delicious to eat, paired with some roasted potatoes or a fresh salad, such as Tomato and Purslane Salad (page 197) or Potato Salad with Capers, Green Beans, and Red Onion (page 201).

IF USING WOODEN skewers, soak them in water for 30 minutes before grilling. Prepare a charcoal or gas grill for direct (medium-high heat) and indirect cooking.

Separate the onion wedges into individual pieces. Before skewering, tuck some of the onions and bay leaves into the sausage coil. Run the skewers crisscrossed through the sausage coil to hold the coil together and make it easier to turn while grilling. Tuck the remaining onion pieces and bay leaves snugly between the skewered coils of the sausage (you may not use all of the onion).

Grill the sausage on the hot side of the grill—turning once and moving to the cooler side of the grill if flare-ups occur—until cooked through, 10 to 15 minutes, depending on the thickness of the sausage.

Remove from the grill, discard the skewers and bay leaves, and cut the sausage into pieces. Serve warm with the onions.

NOTE: The sausage can also be cooked in a grill pan or cast-iron skillet.

MEAT ROLL-UPS

involtini di carne

SERVES 6 TO 8

FOR THE STUFFING

1 small red onion,
finely chopped

2 tablespoons olive oil

4 ounces (115 g) good-quality
firm white sandwich bread,
cut into ¼-inch (6 mm) dice

4 ounces (115 g) provolone,
cut into ¼-inch (6 mm) dice

4 ounces (115 g) prosciutto
cotto or boiled ham, cut into
¼-inch (6 mm) dice

½ cup (20 g) chopped fresh
flat-leaf parsley

1 large egg, lightly beaten

Fine sea salt and freshly
ground black pepper

FOR THE ROLL-UPS

2 pounds (900 g) veal or top
round of beef, cut into about
20 slices ⅛ inch (3 mm) thick

About 1 pound (450 g)
good-quality firm white
sandwich bread, cut into
slices ½ inch (1 cm) thick

½ cup (120 ml) olive oil,
plus more for the baking
sheet

About 24 fresh bay leaves

2 small red onions, cut into
1-inch (2.5 cm) wedges

1½ cups (180 g) plain dried
bread crumbs

EQUIPMENT

12-inch (30 cm) metal or
wooden skewers

Involtini are a must in Sicilian cuisine. These little bundles
are a neat trick: A very thin slice of lean meat stuffed with a
bounty of savory goodies can leave a person happily stuffed
themself. Involtini are great for entertaining, as they can be
assembled well ahead of time and baked just before serving.
They are delicious with roasted potatoes or Potato Salad
with Capers, Green Beans, and Red Onion (page 201).

MAKE THE STUFFING: In a medium skillet, cook the onion in the
olive oil over medium-high heat until just golden, 2 to 3 minutes.
Add the diced bread and toss to coat with olive oil but do not toast.
Remove from the heat and let cool. Add the provolone, prosciutto
cotto, parsley, and egg and mix well. Season with salt and pepper
and set aside.

Prepare the roll-ups: If the meat slices are too thick, use a meat
pounder to pound them to the proper thickness.

Put about 1 heaping tablespoon of stuffing near the bottom
of a slice of meat. Roll the meat over the stuffing, tucking in the
edges to contain the filling, and roll into a small sausage-like shape.
Repeat with the remaining meat and stuffing.

Cut the crusts off the bread slices, then cut the bread into
rectangles about the same length as the meat rolls.

Preheat the oven to 375°F (190°C). Oil a large baking sheet.

Thread 2 skewers about 1 inch (2.5 cm) apart through a meat
roll. Add a bay leaf, a wedge of onion, and a slice of bread. Repeat to
fill the skewers, then continue with the remaining meat rolls, bay
leaves, onions, and bread.

Pour the ½ cup (120 ml) olive oil into a large shallow dish and
place the bread crumbs in another shallow bowl. Dip the filled
skewers in the olive oil and then in the bread crumbs, coating
lightly on all sides. Arrange the skewers on the prepared baking
sheet as you work.

Bake for 10 minutes, then flip the skewers and bake until the
meat is lightly browned and the stuffing is cooked through, 10 to
15 minutes longer.

Remove the involtini, toasted bread, onions, and bay leaves from
the skewers and pile onto a serving platter. Serve warm.

NOTE: Involtini can be assembled and skewered up to 6 hours
ahead, covered in plastic wrap, and refrigerated. Dip in the olive oil
and bread crumbs just before baking.

STREET FOOD

OFFAL AND STREET FOOD ARE NOT NECESSARILY synonymous, but they both come from a condition of famine and extreme poverty, in which the first rule was that nothing could be thrown away. When it came time to butcher an animal, any Sicilian peasant farmer knew to value the offal, which refers to all the bits and pieces you might think to discard—tongue, head, hooves, ears, tail, as well as the organs such as the stomach, lungs, and spleen. And the ways to prepare those odds and ends were infinite, limited only by the imagination of the cook. Most of the offal needs to be boiled first to soften the meat, and then it can be chopped, sautéed in lard, and seasoned with tomato sauce or more simply with olive oil and lemon, such as for u musso, a dish consisting of the ears, snout, and feet of a pig. Tripe can be baked, frittola (scraps left from butchering) will be fried after being boiled, and stigghiole (lamb's intestines wrapped around parsley and onion) will be roasted or grilled.

Many of these dishes have made their way to the big cities of Catania and Palermo and have found huge social value as street food. This food was traditionally eaten solely by men, with their hands, standing in the street. No sitting at a table, no knives and forks. For citizens who did not deal daily and directly with farm animals, these dishes were perhaps in some ways a forbidden food, a rare delicacy only for those with serious stomachs. Now street food is enjoyed equally by all and sought out by adventurous tourists.

SICILIAN MEATLOAF

polpettone

SERVES 8

FOR THE MEATLOAF MIXTURE

5 slices firm white sandwich bread (about 4½ ounces/125 g)

2 tablespoons whole milk

2¼ pounds (1 kg) ground beef or a mixture of ground beef and ground pork

4 large eggs

1 small yellow onion, very finely chopped or grated on a box grater

1 cup (120 g) finely grated Parmigiano-Reggiano or pecorino cheese

1 tablespoon finely chopped fresh flat-leaf parsley leaves

1 tablespoon finely chopped fresh mint

2 teaspoons fine sea salt

1 teaspoon freshly ground black pepper

FOR ASSEMBLY

3½ ounces (100 g) prosciutto cotto or boiled ham, very thinly sliced

½ cup (100 g) boiled, drained, and chopped mustard greens, Swiss chard, or spinach

3½ ounces (100 g) mild provolone cheese or primo sale, very thinly sliced

4 large eggs, hard-boiled and peeled

You won't find polpettone in a Sicilian restaurant—it's definitely home cooking, and every region and cook has their own version. This one is stuffed with thin slices of ham and provolone, cooked greens, and hard-boiled eggs, resulting in a meatloaf slice that is rich and as beautiful as a peacock's feather. The well-seasoned meatloaf mixture itself, without the stuffing, can also be shaped and cooked as meatballs.

PREHEAT THE OVEN to 350°F (180°C). Line a large sheet pan with parchment paper.

Make the meatloaf mixture: Cut off and discard the crusts of the sandwich bread. Cut the bread into small cubes and place in a large bowl. Sprinkle the milk on top and toss to combine. Let sit for 5 minutes to soften.

Add the ground beef, eggs, onion, Parmigiano, parsley, mint, salt, and pepper to the moistened bread. Using your hands, knead and squeeze the ingredients together until they are thoroughly incorporated.

Assemble the meatloaf: Gather up the meat mixture and place it on a large sheet of parchment paper. Use your hands to flatten the mixture into a 12-by-16-inch (30 by 40 cm) rectangle about ½ inch (1 cm) thick. Set the rectangle with a long side facing you.

Lay the ham slices over the meat mixture, covering it almost completely from edge to edge. Distribute the cooked greens evenly over the ham and then top with the cheese slices. Place the hard-boiled eggs end to end in a row running lengthwise down the center. Using the parchment paper to help, lift and wrap the meat, like a jelly roll, over the eggs, and keep rolling until it forms a large sausage. Press the ends together to seal the fillings inside. Transfer the meatloaf to the prepared sheet pan, discarding the parchment used to roll it.

Bake the meatloaf for 30 minutes. Increase the oven temperature to 475°F (250°C) and roast until the outside is browned, 5 to 10 minutes. Remove from the oven and let rest for a few minutes before slicing.

Arrange the slices on a platter and serve hot or at room temperature.

NOTE: The meatloaf can be assembled, wrapped tightly in plastic wrap, and refrigerated for up to 6 hours before baking.

VEGETABLES
verdure

Sicily has an incredible array of vegetables, both farmed and wild. This bounty has allowed generations of peasants living in rural areas to survive when food was scarce, a frequent and very real issue. They took full advantage of the island's wild edible world, knowing how to identify and forage for crisciuni (watercress), scoddi (Spanish oyster thistle), napruddi (Scotch thistle), aprocchi (cornflower), carduna (cardoons), sinapi (wild mustard), borragine (borage), cicoria (wild chicory), cavoliceddi di vigna (wild kale), porcellana (purslane), finocchietto selvatico (wild fennel), and porri (wild leek), among many other plants.

All year round, but especially in early spring, you will see small Fiats parked by the side of the road, their owners inspecting the grassy verge, scampering up nearby hills, or poking in creeks, bags and baskets in hand, seeking to forage anything nature can provide: the wild plants and vegetables listed above, as well as mushrooms, snails, and even, once upon a time, eels and frogs.

Foraging is only the first step in a laborious process that includes cleaning, cooking, and preserving all of these ingredients, a complexity of knowledge that is very much in danger of extinction. The rituals of cleaning and cooking—domesticating the wild, so to speak!—have always been women's work, and Sicilian women from the countryside know just what to keep and what to discard. It is hard work that requires loads of patience, but it can also provide opportunities for the women of the family or village to gather together and socialize while getting necessary chores done.

At the same time, families living in the countryside or on the outskirts of the big cities often have a small backyard garden patch crammed with as many tomato, eggplant, and zucchini plants as possible, as well as a fruit tree or two—apricot, cherry, orange, lemon, or quince. The elderly family members would be the ones to take care of the garden, while, again, the women would come together to make the most of its harvest: jarring tomato sauce and estratto, shelling beans for storage, making fruit preserves, and so much more.

As much as Sicilians love their vegetables, their relationship with raw food is rockier. If you order a salad in a Sicilian restaurant, what you most often receive is a plate of iceberg lettuce topped with some shaved carrots and pale tomato slices, probably from a faraway greenhouse. How can this be, in a place where such delicious things grow?! Well, before widespread refrigeration made it easy to keep foods fresh, Sicilians were suspicious of eating raw food (which was also considered feed for animals). The few vegetables that were eaten raw, such as domestic fennel, onions, and tomatoes, were basically considered fruit. Everything else was boiled, then seasoned very simply with olive oil and lemon juice or sautéed further with olive oil and garlic. Others were cooked more elaborately, like the many layers and textures that go into a caponata.

Today, more people understand that precious minerals can be lost by overcooking vegetables. And, from a gastronomic perspective, a quicker cooking time helps retain the greens' bright emerald color as well as a bit of bite and crunch, a quality that has gained more appreciation in recent years. The concepts of terroir and Slow Food are now quite well regarded in Sicily, and you can find dishes of wild greens served as a local specialty in both high-end restaurants and more rustic trattorias. Despite the gradual disappearance of both wild fields and the people who know how and what to forage, bitter greens are still worshipped by Sicilians. And the forager is celebrated as one who knows what to "hunt" for and when to do so, exploring every single inch of the territory with their eyes, mind, and body, in a wonderful symbiosis with the landscape that so few get to experience anymore.

At the height of summer, eggplants, peppers, and tomatoes fill Sicilian markets.

FENNEL-ORANGE SALAD WITH BLACK OLIVES

insalata finocchio d'arancia con olive

SERVES 4 TO 6

3 medium oranges, preferably blood oranges

1 large fennel bulb

1 cup (180 g) black olives, pitted and halved

6 oil-packed anchovy fillets, chopped

1 teaspoon fresh thyme leaves

¼ teaspoon fine sea salt

Freshly ground black pepper

2 tablespoons extra-virgin olive oil

The time to make this salad is winter, when you can get your hands on the best oranges. Because fennel's anise flavor is naturally sweet, it is important that the oranges be somewhat sour, to provide balance. Blood oranges work beautifully here. This pretty salad makes a fine accompaniment to Roast Chicken with Oranges (page 162), Meat Roll-Ups (page 179), or Breaded Swordfish (page 145).

USING A SMALL sharp knife, cut off the tops and bottoms of the oranges, then continue to cut away the rest of the peel, white pith, and outer membrane to expose the fruit. Cut between the inner membranes to release the segments and place them in a serving bowl.

Cut the fennel bulb into quarters and trim away the core. Slice the fennel quarters into very thin strips and add them to the bowl of orange segments. Mix in the olives, anchovies, thyme, salt, and several grinds of pepper. Drizzle the olive oil over the salad and toss gently to combine. Finish with another pinch of salt and serve at once.

TOMATO AND PURSLANE SALAD

insalata di pomodoro e porcellana

SERVES 6

1 small red onion,
very thinly sliced

Fine sea salt

¼ cup (60 ml) olive oil

2 tablespoons red wine
vinegar

1 small garlic clove, smashed

Freshly ground black pepper

1 pound 5 ounces (600 g)
tomatoes

14 ounces (400 g) fresh
purslane, coarsely chopped

Purslane, a succulent known as porcellana in Italy and purceddana in Sicily, is a hardy weed commonly found growing along the walkways of gardens and even poking out between cracks in cement. Look for it in summer at farmers' markets (or even in your own backyard). Its stems and rounded green leaves are tart, delightfully juicy, and rich in omega-3 fatty acids. Purslane is delicious raw, tossed with tomatoes or boiled potatoes, or cooked and added to omelets. Sicilians generally use oblong Roma-type tomatoes for salads, but cherry or grape tomatoes also work well here.

TOSS THE ONION in a salad bowl with a pinch of salt and let soften for 10 minutes.

In a small bowl, whisk together the olive oil, vinegar, and garlic. Season to taste with salt and pepper.

Cut the tomatoes into bite-size pieces (if using cherry tomatoes, simply halve them), saving the juice, and add both the chopped tomatoes and their juice to the bowl with the sliced onion. Add the purslane.

Drizzle the dressing over the salad and toss gently until just combined. Taste and adjust the seasonings as needed. Serve at once.

ZUCCHINI CARPACCIO

carpaccio di zucchine

SERVES 6

2 pounds (900 g) medium zucchini, trimmed

1¾ ounces (50 g) Parmigiano-Reggiano cheese

1 teaspoon dried oregano, preferably wild (see Resources, page 310)

½ teaspoon fine sea salt

¼ teaspoon freshly ground black pepper

3 tablespoons extra-virgin olive oil

1 or 2 lemons, halved

Most people who live in the Sicilian countryside own a big enough patch of land that they can grow the essentials. Zucchini are a must, and several varieties are commonly grown: cucuzza lunga, a long, snakelike squash (used in Tenerumi Soup, page 70); the pale striped zucchina da friggere, which is often fried and served on pasta; and finally the zucchina verde, which is what we use for this recipe. A lovely and fresh side dish to meats and fish, this recipe reflects Sicilians' relatively newfound enthusiasm for eating raw vegetables.

USING A MANDOLINE or a very sharp knife, slice the zucchini lengthwise as thinly as possible. Arrange the zucchini slices on a serving platter.

Use a vegetable peeler to shave the Parmigiano cheese into thin slivers and scatter over the zucchini. Sprinkle the oregano, salt, and pepper over the salad.

Just before serving, drizzle with the olive oil and add lemon juice to taste. Toss gently to combine and serve at once.

CAPERS

THE CAPER PLANT (*CAPPARIS SPINOSA*) GROWS WILD ALL
over the Mediterranean, especially in unspoiled spots long
abandoned by humans. Ancient ruins are often covered with
huge caper plants cascading from small cracks in the walls.
Despite their ability to flourish in the wild—the plants require very
little water and thrive in fertile volcanic soil—capers have also
been cultivated since ancient times. Today, the most renowned
Sicilian capers come from Pantelleria and Salina. The harvest
happens from May to August, in waves—every eight days or so,
the plant is dotted with new flower buds (i.e., the capers). As with
olives, the buds are unbearably bitter when eaten right from the
plant and must be cured for several days with salt in order to be
palatable. (Sicilians much prefer salt-packed capers to those in a
vinegar brine but know that salted capers need a good rinsing
before using.) After the plant goes to flower, you can collect the
fruit, known as the cucuncio or caperberry, which can also be
cured in salt to make a delightfully crunchy appetizer.

POTATO SALAD WITH
CAPERS, GREEN BEANS, AND RED ONION

insalata patate, capperi, fagiolini, e cipolla rossa

SERVES 6

2¼ pounds (1 kg) waxy potatoes

Fine sea salt

¼ cup (60 ml) white or red wine vinegar

1 small red onion, thinly sliced

1 pound (450 g) green beans, trimmed

½ cup (75 g) salt-packed capers, well rinsed

2 tablespoons olive oil

Freshly ground black pepper

2 tablespoons finely chopped fresh flat-leaf parsley

The combination of buttery potatoes, salty capers, and piquant onions is a happy marriage for Sicilians. Adding green beans makes this a perfect summertime picnic dish to accompany all kinds of delicious grilled meats or fish. Red onions are ideal to use in this potato salad, particularly Tropea onions, because they are generally milder, sweeter, and juicier than the yellow ones. Or if you find fresh spring onions in the market, by all means use them.

IN A POT, combine the potatoes with cold water to cover and salt well. Bring to a boil, then simmer until the potatoes are tender when poked with a fork, 15 to 25 minutes depending on their size. Use a slotted spoon to transfer the potatoes to a colander to cool. (Keep the pot of cooking water.)

When the potatoes are cool enough to handle, peel them and cut into 1-inch (2.5 cm) cubes. Place in a large bowl. Drizzle the vinegar over the still-warm potatoes and toss gently to combine.

Meanwhile, put the onion slices in a bowl of cold water with a large pinch of salt. Let sit for 10 minutes.

Return the pot of cooking water to a boil. Add the green beans and cook until bright green and just tender, 3 to 4 minutes. Drain and let cool.

Drain the onion and add to the bowl of potatoes, along with the capers and blanched green beans. Drizzle the olive oil over everything and season to taste with salt and black pepper. Toss gently to combine.

Garnish the potato salad with the chopped parsley before serving.

NOTE: The potato salad can be made up to 8 hours ahead and refrigerated.

HONEY-ROASTED FENNEL AND CARDOONS

finocchi e cardi al miele

SERVES 6

Fine sea salt

2 lemons

1 pound (450 g) cardoons
(see Note)

1 medium red onion,
halved and thinly sliced

2 fennel bulbs,
cored and thinly sliced

2 tablespoons olive oil

2 tablespoons dry white wine

3 tablespoons honey, plus
more for drizzling

1 tablespoon fresh thyme
leaves

Freshly ground black pepper

¼ cup (30 g) toasted
pine nuts

Fried cardoons drizzled with honey is a traditional dish often made in central Sicily for the Feast of Saint Joseph. In the past, wild cardoons, which can be very bitter, were most likely used, with the honey added for balance. This updated dish adds fennel and onions to the mix and forgoes the fryer for the oven. It makes a fine accompaniment to Roast Pork with Mint and Garlic (page 175) or the Lamb-Stuffed Pastry (page 169).

BRING A LARGE pot of salted water to a boil. Cut 1 of the lemons in half and squeeze the juice into the pot, then drop in the squeezed halves. Trim and peel the cardoons, discarding any tough or fibrous bits. Cut them crosswise into 4-inch (10 cm) lengths. Add the trimmed cardoons to the boiling water, reduce the heat slightly, and boil until tender when poked with a fork, 30 to 40 minutes.

Preheat the oven to 400°F (200°C).

Drain the cardoons, let them cool slightly, then slice them lengthwise into batons ½ inch (1 cm) wide. Place the sliced cardoons in a large bowl and add the onion and fennel.

In a small bowl, whisk together the olive oil, wine, honey, half of the thyme leaves, and 2 tablespoons of juice from the remaining lemon. Drizzle the mixture over the sliced vegetables and toss well to coat. Season with salt and pepper. Spread the vegetables on a sheet pan or in a baking dish.

Roast, stirring occasionally, until the fennel and onion are tender and everything is beginning to caramelize, about 30 minutes.

Remove from the oven and transfer to a serving platter. Drizzle a little more honey over the vegetables and sprinkle the pine nuts and remaining thyme leaves on top. Mix gently to combine before serving warm or at room temperature.

NOTE: The cardoons can be peeled and boiled up to 1 day ahead. Refrigerate, covered. And if you can't find cardoons, omit the boiling step and simply add a third fennel bulb.

STUFFED ARTICHOKES

carciofi alla frocia

SERVES 6 TO 8

2 lemons, halved

10 medium artichokes

Fine sea salt

1⅔ cups (200 g) plain
dried bread crumbs

2½ ounces (75 g) pecorino
cheese, finely grated

2 tablespoons finely
chopped fresh flat-leaf
parsley

1 tablespoon finely
chopped fresh mint

3 large eggs

½ medium onion,
finely chopped

Freshly ground black pepper

Olive oil, for frying

Artichokes were imported to Sicily by the Arab conquerors and likely spread from there to the rest of Italy. With a number of different varieties growing all over the island, Sicily is now the second-largest producer of artichokes in the country. The spinoso artichoke from Menfi has bright golden thorns and is excellent for grilling. It is a Slow Food Presidium (see page 210). The violetto siciliano is possibly the most common in all the southeast, while the violetto di Castellammare, also a Slow Food Presidium, is rounder and thornless, similar to the mammole artichoke from central Italy. Not surprisingly, artichokes are a common ingredient in many Sicilian recipes. Here the vegetable is stuffed with seasoned bread crumbs and fried. These tender, savory morsels are delicious just as they are, but you could also add an extra layer of flavor by gently simmering the artichokes in a pan of tomato sauce after they have been fried.

SQUEEZE THE JUICE of the lemons into a large bowl of cold water. Add the spent lemon rinds.

Trim the artichokes down to the tender leaves, halve lengthwise, and scoop out the fuzzy choke. As you work, drop the cleaned artichokes into the bowl of water and lemon.

Bring a large pot of salted water to a boil, add the artichokes, and simmer gently until tender, 10 to 15 minutes. Drain well and let cool.

Meanwhile, in a large bowl, combine the bread crumbs, pecorino, parsley, mint, eggs, and onion to make a stiff, sticky mixture. Season well with salt and pepper. Stuff a small handful of the mixture into the cavity of each artichoke, gently packing it in to make it stick.

Line a sheet pan with paper towels. Pour 1 inch (2.5 cm) of olive oil into a large heavy skillet and heat over medium heat until shimmering. Working in batches if necessary, place as many artichokes as will fit, filling-side down, in the hot oil and cook until the filling is well browned, about 5 minutes. Flip and cook for another 2 to 3 minutes.

Transfer to the paper towels to drain. Serve warm.

NOTE: The artichokes can be prepped and filled up to 6 hours in advance and kept refrigerated. Gently reheat leftovers in a bit of olive oil on the stove (or microwave them).

SLOW FOOD PRESIDIA

STARTED IN ITALY'S PIEDMONT IN 1986 AS A PROTEST AGAINST
the hectic nature of modern life, the Slow Food movement
promotes the pleasure of conviviality, the value of thoughtfully
grown food, the hard work of farmers and producers, and good
home cooking. The Slow Food Presidia project, started in 2000,
evolved as a way to protect and promote small-scale producers
struggling against industrial agriculture. These producers
work to rescue indigenous breeds, preserve biodiversity, and
safeguard traditional food production techniques. In the process,
they educate consumers about landscapes, terroirs, and local
cultures. Today, there are nearly six hundred fifty Presidia all over
the world in seventy-nine different countries. Among the Italian
regions, Sicily has the largest number of Presidia, representing
everything from the sesame seed of Ispica to several types of
cheeses, vegetables, honey, fruits, and sausages—an astonishing
breadth that demonstrates the island's incredible biodiversity
and rich food culture.

GREEN BEANS WITH ANCHOVIES AND BREAD CRUMBS

fagiolini ripassati

SERVES 4 TO 6

Fine sea salt

2 pounds (900 g) green beans

2 anchovy fillets, rinsed if salt-packed

⅓ cup (80 ml) olive oil

3 garlic cloves, finely chopped

Freshly ground black pepper

½ cup (60 g) plain dried bread crumbs

Preserved anchovies are often used as a base for sauces or condiments, and as such they are considered less a fish and more a seasoning that adds umami and deep flavor to everything they touch. Here sweet and tender green beans get a salty boost from anchovies and crunch from toasted bread crumbs.

BRING A LARGE pot of lightly salted water to a boil.

While the water heats up, trim the stem end of each green bean, but leave the tender little tail end attached.

Cook the green beans in the boiling water until bright green but not quite tender, about 3 minutes. Drain in a colander.

In a large skillet, cook the anchovies in the olive oil over medium-high heat for 1 minute, using a wooden spoon to break them up. Add the green beans and garlic and cook, stirring occasionally, until the beans are tender, 5 to 7 minutes. Remove the pan from the heat. Season with salt and pepper (remember that the anchovies will have already given a bit of salt to the dish).

Add the bread crumbs to the green beans and toss gently to combine, letting them soak up some of the olive oil, and toast for a moment in the still-hot pan. Serve warm.

EGGPLANT CAPONATA

caponata di melanzane

SERVES 8 TO 10 AS A
SIDE DISH

Fine sea salt

**1 small head celery, tough
outer stalks discarded,
strings removed, sliced**

Vegetable oil, for frying

**2¼ pounds (1 kg) firm
eggplant, peeled and cut
into 1-inch (2.5 cm) cubes**

**1 large onion, halved and
sliced lengthwise**

¼ cup (60 ml) olive oil

**1 cup (180 g) green olives,
pitted and cut into thirds**

**⅓ cup (40 g) salt-packed
capers, rinsed**

**1½ cups (360 ml) good-
quality tomato sauce,
homemade (page 87)
or store-bought**

**¼ cup (60 ml) red or white
wine vinegar**

**1 tablespoon sugar,
plus more as needed**

**Chopped fresh flat-leaf
parsley, for garnish**

Caponata is basically a cooked salad made with the most classic of Mediterranean ingredients: eggplants, tomatoes, olives, capers, and olive oil. You can find variations of this type of dish all over this part of the world—think French ratatouille, Spanish pisto, or Israeli eggplant salatim—and, it must be said, almost as many different versions of caponata within Sicily as there are Sicilians. But caponata's sweet-and-sour seasoning sets it apart, as does its architectural nature, meaning each main ingredient should be cooked separately and then gently folded together so that its various flavors and textures remain distinct. In winter, when eggplants are less available, caponata can be made with sautéed artichokes. Caponata used to be served only among antipasti, but today it is often served as a side dish to meat, fish, or cheese.

BRING A SMALL saucepan of salted water to a boil. Add the celery and cook until bright green, 1 to 2 minutes. Drain.

Pour at least 2 inches (5 cm) of vegetable oil into a wide heavy-bottomed pot and heat over medium-high heat until it is hot enough to fry in (see Deep-Frying, page 30). Line a large plate with paper towels.

Once the oil is ready, carefully lower as many eggplant cubes as will fit without crowding into the hot oil. Fry, flipping occasionally, until golden brown and tender, 5 to 6 minutes. Use a slotted spoon to transfer the fried eggplant to the paper towels to drain. Sprinkle with salt. Repeat to fry the remaining eggplant cubes.

In a large pan, sauté the onion in the olive oil over medium heat until just golden, about 5 minutes. Add the blanched celery, olives, capers, tomato sauce, vinegar, and sugar. Taste and season with salt and another pinch of sugar if the mixture is too tart. Gently fold in the eggplant, being careful not to smash the cubes. Simmer for 2 to 3 minutes, then transfer to a large bowl or platter and let cool.

Sprinkle chopped parsley over the caponata and serve at room temperature or chilled.

NOTE: Caponata tastes even better the next day. If you have leftovers, tuck them into sandwiches or eat with fried eggs.

SOILS

ORANGE, RED, WHITE, YELLOW, BLACK—THESE ARE JUST SOME of the beautiful colors of Sicilian soil. Every corner of the island has its own specific dirt—composed of clay, sand, seashells, limestone, fossils, mud, silt, lava—that contributes to building a sense of place and a basis for unique flavor compounds that can range from salty to mineral, bitter, and acidic. Sloped hills that have more erosion tend to have shallow, yellowish-gray soil; the wide large plains surrounding Catania and Palermo are mostly made out of sand and clay residue from alluvial deposits; the southeast is white with limestone; central Sicily tends to be red with clay and streaked with pink where it mixes with sand; while Etna and most of the small islands surrounding Sicily exhibit an incredible array of black soils coming from lava deposits.

Sicily is still quite a "shaky" land, the result of a clash between the African and Eurasian tectonic plates millions of years ago, which created several volcanoes and salt caves. This unsettled nature means there is still regular volcanic activity on land, while below sea those movements translate into millions of gas bubbles that create hot springs.

A good example of volcanic soil—incredibly rich and fertile and either sandy or stony, according to its lava age—is found on the eighteen small islands grouped in a handful of archipelagos around Sicily. The largest of them is Pantelleria, the "black pearl of the Mediterranean," halfway between southeastern Sicily and Tunisia, which is also where you'll find the three Pelagie Islands: Lampedusa, Linosa, and Lampione. The Aeolian Islands are stationed off the northern coast. Ustica floats alone north of Palermo, and the Egadi Islands face Trapani. The volcanoes Stromboli and Vulcano are still active, as is Etna, whose nickname is Mongibello, or "majestic mountain." Any fruit or vegetable grown on this black, uneven soil bears an intensity of flavor that is unique in all of Sicily.

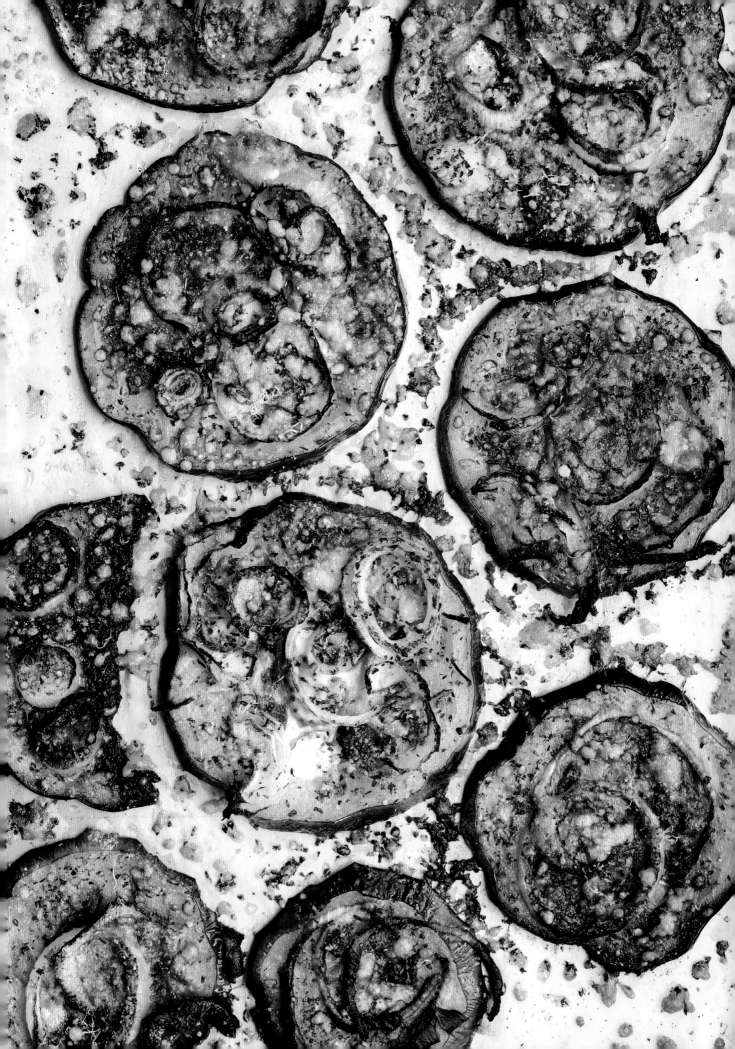

BAKED EGGPLANT

melanzane al forno

SERVES 4 TO 6

**2 large firm eggplants
(about 2¼ pounds/1 kg)**

**1 medium yellow onion,
thinly sliced**

**6 to 8 oil-packed anchovy
fillets, torn into pieces**

**¼ cup (25 g) finely grated
Parmigiano-Reggiano cheese**

**1 tablespoon dried
oregano, preferably wild
(see Resources, page 310)**

¾ cup (180 ml) olive oil

**Fine sea salt and freshly
ground black pepper**

Eggplant makes frequent appearances on the Sicilian table. Farmers are experimenting with more and more varieties these days, but most common are the big purple globes known as Tunisina and the classic ebony-hued oblong variety, which is typically used for caponata and eggplant Parmesan. To make this baked eggplant, choose a variety that is firm, fresh, and in season.

PREHEAT THE OVEN to 350°F (180°C). Line two large sheet pans with parchment paper.

Cut the eggplants crosswise into slices ½ inch (1 cm) thick and arrange on the prepared pans.

Scatter the onion, anchovies, Parmigiano, and oregano over the eggplant and drizzle with the olive oil. Season lightly with salt and pepper.

Roast until the eggplant is golden and tender, about 40 minutes. Serve hot or warm.

BAKED CAULIFLOWER WITH BLACK OLIVES AND CHEESE

cavolfiore con olive nere e formaggio

SERVES 6

½ cup (120 ml) olive oil,
plus 1 tablespoon for the pan

Fine sea salt

2 medium heads cauliflower,
cut into large florets

1 small yellow onion,
very finely chopped

Freshly ground black pepper

8 ounces (225 g) primo sale,
tuma, or provola cheese,
sliced

½ cup (100 g) black olives,
pitted and halved

Cauliflower, known as cavolfiore in most of Italy, is commonly (and confusingly, for some) called broccoli in Sicily. There are two main varieties of cauliflower in Sicilian cuisine—the bright green one, which is traditionally grown and eaten around Palermo, and a dark purple variety called violetto di Sicilia that is popular in the area surrounding Catania. Both have very distinctive properties—the purple being rounder and sweeter, and the green more pungent and savory. Either variety, or common white cauliflower, works well here. This is not meant to be a saucy dish—each ingredient should hold on to its individual taste and texture. Because you want a cheese that remains quite firm during baking, primo sale or tuma, both sheep's-milk cheeses, are generally used here, but a mild provolone or lightly salted mozzarella also works well.

PREHEAT THE OVEN to 375°F (190°C). Oil a 9-by-13-inch (23 by 33 cm) baking pan with the 1 tablespoon olive oil.

Bring a large pot of well-salted water to a boil. Add the cauliflower and cook until crisp-tender but not at all mushy, about 5 minutes. Drain well, then spread the cauliflower in the prepared baking pan.

In a medium skillet, cook the onion in ¼ cup (60 ml) of the olive oil over medium heat, stirring often, until softened, 2 to 3 minutes. Remove the pan from the heat and scatter the onions over the cauliflower florets. Season lightly with salt and pepper, keeping in mind that the olives and the cheese will add quite a bit of saltiness. Drape the sliced cheese over the cauliflower, then scatter the olives on top. Drizzle the remaining ¼ cup (60 ml) olive oil over everything.

Bake until the top is nice and golden, 20 to 30 minutes. Serve warm or at room temperature.

NOTE: The dish can be assembled up to 6 hours in advance of baking and refrigerated.

SPINACH FLAN

flan di spinaci

SERVES 8

2 tablespoons (30 g) unsalted butter, plus more for the pan

Fine sea salt

2¼ pounds (1 kg) spinach

3 tablespoons all-purpose flour

1 cup (240 ml) whole milk

⅔ cup (170 g) whole-milk ricotta cheese

5 tablespoons (30 g) grated Parmigiano-Reggiano or pecorino cheese

Pinch of freshly grated nutmeg

3 large eggs, lightly beaten

The idea of adding ricotta to a béchamel-based flan comes directly from the French-Sicilian alphabet of monsù cuisine (see page 152). Spinach is a natural addition, but almost any kind of leafy green, such as Swiss chard or chicory, can be substituted. Serve this tender flan with Double-Crust Swordfish Pie (page 150) or Braised Rabbit with Black Olives and Rosemary (page 167).

PREHEAT THE OVEN to 350°F (180°C). Butter a flan mold or a 7-inch (18 cm) round baking pan 3 inches (7 cm) deep.

Bring a large pot of salted water to a boil. Add the spinach and cook until wilted and tender, about 4 minutes. Transfer the spinach to a colander to drain. When it's cool enough to handle, squeeze the spinach well to remove as much water as possible. In a food processor or blender, blend the cooked spinach to a smooth puree.

In a medium saucepan, combine the 2 tablespoons (30 g) butter, flour, and milk and cook over medium-high heat, whisking constantly, until thickened, about 5 minutes. Remove from the heat and whisk in the ricotta, Parmigiano, nutmeg, and pureed spinach. Season to taste with salt. Add the eggs and mix well. Pour into the prepared flan mold.

Place the filled mold in a larger baking pan and set the pan on a pulled-out oven rack. Pour enough boiling-hot water into the larger pan so that it reaches halfway up the sides of the mold. Bake the flan until just set, 35 to 40 minutes. Let cool slightly before inverting onto a serving platter. Serve warm.

NOTE: The flan mixture can be made up to 2 hours before baking. Refrigerate it until ready to use.

PIZZA AND BREAD

pizza e pane

FRIED CALZONE 230
calzone fritto

**SCACCIA FROM RAGUSA
WITH TOMATOES AND BASIL 235**
scaccia ragusana con pomodori e basilico

**STUFFED PIZZA FROM MODICA
WITH GREENS AND CHEESE 239**
impanata di modica con cicorie e formaggio

PALERMITAN PIZZA 242
sfincione

**FOCACCIA WITH BLACK OLIVES AND
ROSEMARY 249**
focaccia con olive nere e rosmarino

**FOCACCIA FROM MESSINA
WITH ESCAROLE AND TOMATOES 250**
focaccia messinese con scarola e pomodori

CHRISTMAS SFOGLIO FROM RAGUSA 254
sfoglio di natale di ragusa

Bread is at the heart of the meal for any Sicilian, who would not sit at the table without having a loaf of bread ready to eat with everything—meat, soup, cheese, pasta. Until the 1960s, bread, wine, and something to go with it—a hunk of cheese or a few salted sardines—was the meager pay many workers received for a day's labor. The relationship between the fields waving their golden tassels of wheat and the farmers harvesting and milling it into flour was, and still is, strong. Likewise, the connection between lunch and landscape has always been very close, especially in central Sicily, where the land was in the hands of so few owners, and wheat was the main crop, for so many centuries. Not surprisingly, bread has a very strong symbolic value for Sicilians, and there is no feast-day celebration that doesn't come with a specific shape of bread.

Nowadays very few people still bake in wood-burning ovens, and bakeries often use enriched flours that are not produced in Sicily; therefore you need to go to specific areas to still find a true Sicilian loaf—a compact, doughy bread with no airy holes to mar its cakelike slice. Piana degli Albanesi and Monreale near Palermo are two such places, along with a few small villages around the island, such as Polizzi Generosa in the Madonie Mountains and other bigger cities such as Catania, where there is a demand and a willingness to pay more to get bread made with local flour.

Fortunately, a new sensibility toward landraces has been growing in the last twenty years. Sicily has, in its long history, grown an incredible variety of cultivars, and these older grains, displaced over time by industrial flours, are now making a comeback, thanks in part to both a growing understanding of gluten sensitivity and a reappreciation of their more complex flavors and aromas.

The main wheat variety grown in Sicily is durum (*Triticum durum*), used for pasta and bread, which is quite different from soft wheat (*Triticum aestivum*), sown in very small quantities and used mainly for baking biscuits and cakes. It is a matter of soil—durum wheat grows very well in dry climates with clayish soil (e.g., Sicily), while soft wheat prefers wet, rainy plains, such as those found in Northern Italy. The flour made from durum wheat, better known in the United States as semolina, has a somewhat coarse, sandy texture and a yellow tint (from the presence of carotene), while flour from soft wheat is white and powdery. Most American semolinas are even coarser than their Sicilian counterparts. Whenever possible, look for imported semolina (see Resources, page 310).

Small producers, millers, and pasta makers are now scattered around the island producing semolina flour. Bidì, Russello, Margherito, Bufala Nera, and Perciasacchi are some of the heritage grains that are regaining popularity in Sicily and are being used for bread as well as for pasta. Flour made from the ancient wheat Tumminia is the main ingredient for Castelvetrano "black" bread, now a Slow Food Presidium (see page 210), while Russello wheat is used to make pasta and breads in the Iblean area of southeast Sicily.

Many Sicilian pizzas call for rimacinata flour to make their doughs. Rimacinata is not, as many believe, a type of flour, but rather just semolina flour that has been milled twice. It produces a very different kind of pizza from the traditional Neapolitan pie, which is always made with a soft, all-purpose flour. And even if the concept may sound similar—a risen dough quickly cooked in a brick oven and eaten as easy, informal food—Sicilian "pizzas" are more closely related to bread. They might be called fuata in Caltanissetta, vastedda in Enna, scaccia in Ragusa and Catania, or sfincione in the Palermitan area, but all are basically a type of bread either topped or stuffed with different seasonings, which can vary according to the area and the season: You'll likely find lots of pork sausage in the area around Ragusa and Noto; vegetables, including the beautiful purple cauliflower, in Catania; and tomato sauce with pecorino and anchovies in Palermo.

FRIED CALZONE

calzone fritto

2 teaspoons active dry yeast

2 tablespoons sugar

1¼ cups (300 ml) lukewarm water

4 cups (480 g) all-purpose flour, plus more for shaping

2 tablespoons lard

1½ teaspoons fine sea salt

Filling options: thin slices of prosciutto cotto and mozzarella, tomato sauce and ricotta cheese, salami and béchamel

Vegetable oil, for frying

Calzone, which can be baked (calzone al forno) or fried (calzone fritto), are sold in rosticcerie (see page 233). The hearty stuffed breads have traditionally been filled with sliced ham, béchamel, and mozzarella, but now you can find them with many variations, such as tomato sauce and mozzarella, prosciutto and fresh tomatoes, and so on. The dough is fluffy, airy, and slightly sweet, similar to a French brioche (which is also the basis for brioche con gelato, another popular snack Sicilians enjoy during the day), and a good reminder of how some aspects of the elaborate French cuisine of the 1800s has evolved and traveled from the noble palaces to the everyday life of the Sicilian streets.

IN A SMALL bowl, mix together the yeast, 1 tablespoon of the sugar, and ¼ cup (60 ml) of the water. Set aside at room temperature until creamy, about 5 minutes. If the yeast doesn't bubble at all, throw it out and start over with new yeast.

In a stand mixer fitted with a dough hook, combine the flour, lard, salt, yeast mixture, remaining 1 tablespoon sugar, and remaining 1 cup (240 ml) water. Mix on low speed until smooth and elastic, about 5 minutes. Cover the bowl with plastic wrap or a clean kitchen towel and let the dough rise in a warm, draft-free place until doubled in size, about 1 hour.

Turn the dough out onto a lightly floured work surface. Divide it into 12 equal portions (each about 75 g) and roll into balls. Use a rolling pin to flatten each ball into a 6-inch (15 cm) round.

Place the filling of your choice on one side of each round—a couple of slices of prosciutto cotto or salami, a thick slice of mozzarella, a spoonful of tomato sauce or ricotta. Fold the other side over to create a half-moon shape, and pinch firmly to seal the edge. (Sealing the dough is the most important step, so that the calzones don't pop open while they are frying.)

Cover the filled calzones with a clean kitchen towel and let rise again in a warm, draft-free place until the dough feels bouncy to the touch, 30 minutes to 1 hour.

Pour at least 2 inches (5 cm) of vegetable oil into a wide heavy-bottomed pot and heat over medium-high heat until it is hot enough to fry in (see Deep-Frying, page 30). Line a sheet pan with paper towels.

Once the oil is ready, slip a few calzones into the hot oil (work in batches to avoid crowding the pot) and fry, carefully flipping them occasionally, until dark golden brown all over, about 4 minutes. Transfer to the paper towels to drain. Repeat with the remaining calzones. Serve warm.

NOTE: Leftover fried calzones can be reheated on a baking sheet in a warm oven.

ROSTICCERIA

IN SICILY, A ROSTICCERIA IS A CASUAL SHOP WHERE
customers can pick up a snack or quick lunch, a coffee, and a
little sweet. The name comes from the French *rôtir*, meaning "to
roast on a spit," a fixture in kitchens since the Middle Ages. After
the French Revolution, private chefs fled to Paris and opened
public restaurants, where a cook called the chef rôtisseur
became responsible for all grilled, spit-roasted, and oven-
roasted meats. In time, this tradition trickled down to Sicily, where
rosticcerie began popping up in bigger cities and evolved to sell
individual servings of baked or fried food that could be taken
home or easily eaten standing up in the store. With no need for
tables, forks, or knives, this was some of the earliest fast food.

Not to be confused with street food, the pezzi da rosticceria
("pieces of rosticceria") include all kinds of pizzettes and calzones
topped or stuffed with ham, salami, cheese, béchamel, tomatoes,
würstel (hot dogs), greens, and other goodies. The doughs
used to make these treats can range from very simple to more
elaborate, fluffy brioches and may be baked or fried depending
on the recipe, the filling, and the location.

You can see a rosticceria on almost every block in Palermo
and Catania, but it's worth exploring those in the smaller towns,
too, where you can find such regional specialties as the pitone
from Messina, a fried calzone filled with escarole, tomatoes,
anchovies, and pecorino; the cuddurini of Lentini near Siracusa,
a half-moon traditionally filled with broccoli and onions and
baked; and the fuata from Caltanissetta, a flatbread topped
with tomatoes, anchovies, and oregano, similar to the Palermitan
Pizza (page 242). The mbriulata from Milena is a crisp puff-pastry
spiral that can be filled with spinach, cheese, olives, pine nuts,
raisins, anchovies, and tomato, while the ranza e sciura, from the
hilltop town of Chiusa Sclafani, is a focaccia topped with onions,
anchovies, and oregano.

FAT

LARD—KNOWN AS *STRUTTO* IN ITALIAN AND *SUGNA* IN SICILIAN
dialect—has always been used in Sicily for all kinds of baking
and some frying. Cannoli were traditionally fried in lard, as was
the spleen in the classic street food sandwich panino con la
milza. Lard started out as an inexpensive option, a way to use
up every aspect of the family pig (olive oil was more often sold
than saved for household use, and butter was out of reach for
most). Rendering pork fat is quite easy: Cook it gently over low
heat until it melts and liquefies, then strain it and store in jars. As
it cools, it will solidify to a creamy white with the consistency
of butter. Whether you render your own lard or buy it ready to
go, it is worth seeking out lard from pasture-raised pigs. Leaf
lard, from around the kidneys, is especially prized for its delicate
flavor and creaminess. Today, lard is used for breads and
pastries like Christmas Sfoglio from Ragusa (page 254) and the
cookies known as taralli (see Knotted Lemon Cookies, page 284);
it provides a particular crunch and flakiness that neither butter
nor olive oil can replicate.

SCACCIA FROM RAGUSA WITH TOMATOES AND BASIL

scaccia ragusana con pomodori e basilico

-photo page 224-

SERVES 4 TO 6

1 teaspoon active dry yeast

½ teaspoon sugar

¾ cup (180 ml) lukewarm water

1½ cups (240 g) semolina flour, plus more for rolling

½ teaspoon fine sea salt

1 cup (240 ml) good-quality tomato sauce, homemade (page 87) or store-bought

½ cup (10 g) fresh basil leaves

1 tablespoon olive oil

A typical stuffed bread from Ragusa, this scaccia is made up of many alternating layers of thin semolina dough and a filling. This is a simple version, made just with tomato sauce and fresh basil leaves, but you could add ricotta, crumbled sausage, pecorino, or caciocavallo. Adding other fillings makes it slightly trickier to fold the dough without breaking it, but even if the dough rips or some sauce drips out, the scaccia will still be delicious!

IN A SMALL bowl, mix together the yeast, sugar, and 2 tablespoons of the water. Set aside at room temperature until creamy, about 5 minutes. If the yeast doesn't bubble at all, throw it out and start over with new yeast.

In a large bowl, mix together the semolina, salt, yeast mixture, and the remaining water. Transfer the dough to a work surface and knead until firm and smooth, about 8 minutes. Shape into a ball and cover with a clean kitchen towel. Let rise in a warm, draft-free place until doubled in size, about 1 hour.

Preheat the oven to 425°F (220°C). Line a baking sheet with parchment paper.

Generously dust the work surface with semolina. Using a rolling pin, roll the dough out into a very thin rectangle about 16 by 24 inches (40 by 61 cm).

With a 16-inch (40 cm) side facing you, spread a thin layer of tomato sauce evenly over the center third of the dough. Sprinkle some basil over the sauce. Fold the bottom third of the dough over the filling, spread a thin layer of sauce across the folded dough, and add a few basil leaves. Fold the top third of the dough over the filling, spread a thin layer of sauce across the newly folded dough, and add some basil leaves. Fold the left third over to the center, spread another thin layer of tomato sauce on the newly folded dough, and add the remaining basil leaves. Finally, fold the right third over the top. The finished scaccia should be roughly 6 by 9 inches (15 by 23 cm). Transfer to the prepared baking sheet, with the folded side on the bottom. Drizzle with the olive oil.

Bake until golden brown, 30 to 35 minutes. Remove from the oven and cover with a clean kitchen towel. Let cool for at least 30 minutes before slicing.

SESAME SEEDS
AND POPPY SEEDS

THE PRESENCE OF SESAME SEEDS IN SICILY DATES BACK TO THE
time of the Greeks, who used them to prepare a ritual cake
during Thesmophoria, the celebration honoring Demeter, the
goddess of wheat. Today, most Sicilian breads are covered
with sesame seeds, which are called giuggiulena or ciminu, or
poppy seeds, known as paparina. Sesame seeds are also used
during fairs and saints' festivals to make a type of brittle with
honey, sugar, and orange zest called cubaita. Even though the
plant has been in Sicily for so long, the production of sesame has
been mostly forgotten, and today the only place still cultivating
it and producing sesame seeds is Ispica, a small town in the
southeastern part of the island. Now a Slow Food Presidium
(see page 210), Ispica's sesame seeds are small and intensely
flavored. The harvest happens at the end of August and requires
a lot of skill—the pods must be carefully collected before they
open, then the seeds need to be sifted—which is probably one of
the reasons why the practice has been nearly abandoned.

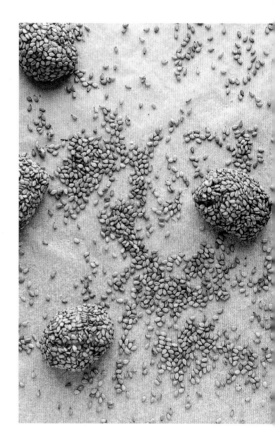

The use of poppy seeds is less common than it once was,
perhaps because the European Union has tried to ban private
individuals from cultivating the plant (in addition to topping
breads, poppy seeds were once used to make tinctures to help
colicky babies sleep). But at one time, most Sicilians had a few
poppy flowers growing in the backyard or in a corner of the
vegetable garden, their beautiful orange or pink blooms waving
behind the broccoli. When the petals fell in June, the poppy plants
were harvested and hung upside down in a shady spot until the
seeds were dry enough to extract from the pods to be stored for
the year to come.

STUFFED PIZZA FROM MODICA WITH GREENS AND CHEESE

impanata di modica con cicorie e formaggio

-photo page 236-

SERVES 4

1 teaspoon active dry yeast

¼ teaspoon sugar

½ cup (120 ml) lukewarm water

1½ cups (240 g) semolina flour

3 tablespoons olive oil

1 teaspoon fine sea salt

½ cup (125 g) whole-milk ricotta cheese

1 cup (140 g) cooked wild chicories or other cooked greens, such as chard, escarole, or broccoli rabe

3 ounces (80 g) primo sale or tuma cheese, thinly sliced

1 large egg, lightly beaten

2 teaspoons sesame seeds

Like many scaccias and pizzas, this half-moon-shaped dough from Modica can be stuffed with anything you like. This particular combination of cooked wild greens, creamy ricotta, and salty primo sale cheese is a winter treat, when all of these ingredients are at their peak in Sicily.

IN A SMALL bowl, mix together the yeast, sugar, and 2 tablespoons of the water. Set aside at room temperature until creamy, about 5 minutes. If the yeast doesn't bubble at all, throw it out and start over with new yeast.

In a large bowl, combine the semolina, olive oil, salt, yeast mixture, and the remaining water and mix until thoroughly combined. Transfer the dough to a work surface and knead until it comes together into a smooth, springy ball, 8 to 10 minutes. Place in the bowl, cover with a clean kitchen towel, and let rise in a warm, draft-free place until doubled in size, about 1 hour.

Preheat the oven to 400°F (200°C). Line a baking sheet with parchment paper.

Use a rolling pin to roll out the dough into a 14-inch (36 cm) round. Spread the ricotta over one half of the dough, leaving a 1-inch (2.5 cm) border. Top the ricotta with the cooked greens and slices of primo sale. Fold the dough over to make a half-moon shape and seal with a fork. Place on the prepared baking sheet. Brush the beaten egg over the dough and sprinkle the sesame seeds on top.

Bake until golden brown, about 20 minutes. Remove from the oven, cover with a clean kitchen towel, and let rest for at least 30 minutes before slicing and serving.

WHEAT

KNOWN AS THE BREADBASKET OF THE ROMAN EMPIRE, THE
vast rolling hills nestled between the provinces of Enna and
Caltanissetta provided wheat for much of Europe well into the
twentieth century. For almost fifteen hundred years the wheat
grown here helped sustain this rural population, while lining
the pockets of the Sicilian aristocrats who owned the land.
These large estates devoted to growing grains and worked by
the local peasants were called latifundia. To this day, the area
remains immense and desolate, just fields and fields of wheat
with not a soul or town in sight for miles. Through winter and
spring, the hills and fields are brightly green and lush. Come
June, they become beautifully golden. Once the wheat is
threshed, the land turns brown and then black in places where
farmers illegally burn it, to clean up the fields and add some
nutrients to the soil.

Scattered across this lunar landscape are big mansions
called bagli or masserie. These square, two-story buildings are
built around a large interior courtyard. The owner used the few
rooms above while the workers, animals, and tools shared the
downstairs space next to huge barns that stored the wheat.
Functioning more like a fortress than an Italian countryside villa,
the masseria embodied the harshness and remoteness of the
landscape as well as the need to be completely self-sufficient.

PALERMITAN PIZZA

sfincione

SERVES 6 TO 8

FOR THE DOUGH

1½ teaspoons active dry yeast

1½ teaspoons sugar

¾ cup plus 2 tablespoons (210 ml) lukewarm water

2 cups (240 g) all-purpose flour

½ cup (80 g) semolina flour

1½ teaspoons fine sea salt

2 tablespoons olive oil, plus more for the pan

FOR THE TOPPING

1 small red onion, thinly sliced

5 tablespoons olive oil

1½ cups (360 ml) good-quality tomato sauce, homemade (page 87) or store-bought

½ cup (60 g) plain dried bread crumbs

8 to 10 oil-packed anchovy fillets, chopped

1 teaspoon dried oregano, preferably wild (see Resources, page 310)

½ cup (60 g) finely grated pecorino cheese

The town of Bagheria, half an hour from Palermo, claims to be the birthplace of sfincione, a thick, spongy pizza topped with anchovies, cheese, bread crumbs, tomato sauce, and oregano. It is greasy, filling—and delicious! A bakery in the old part of Palermo turns out hundreds of sfincioni every day for the many street vendors who sell them from motorized carts—usually a three-wheeled Piaggio Ape that has been outfitted with a glass case at one end and a small oven for reheating the pizzas. Not surprisingly, these carts are a popular destination for kids on their midmorning break from school. But one could argue that sfincione tastes even better fresh from the oven, in the comfort of your own home, and accompanied by a cold beer.

MAKE THE DOUGH: In a small bowl, mix together the yeast, ½ teaspoon of the sugar, and 2 tablespoons of the water. Set aside at room temperature until creamy, about 5 minutes. If the yeast doesn't bubble at all, throw it out and start over with new yeast.

In a large bowl, combine the all-purpose flour, semolina flour, salt, remaining 1 teaspoon sugar, the yeast mixture, and remaining ¾ cup (180 ml) water. Mix well, then add the olive oil and knead it in until fully incorporated. Transfer the dough to a clean work surface and knead until smooth, about 8 minutes. The dough should be soft and pliable. Shape into a ball, place in the bowl, cover with a clean kitchen towel, and let rise in a warm, draft-free place until almost doubled in size, about 1 hour.

Meanwhile, make the topping: Bring a small pot of water to a boil. Add the onion and cook for 3 minutes. Drain.

In a saucepan, cook the blanched onion in 3 tablespoons of the olive oil over medium-low heat, stirring occasionally, until tender and golden, 8 to 10 minutes. Add the tomato sauce and continue cooking until the onion softens completely, about 3 minutes.

In a small bowl, mix together the bread crumbs, anchovies, ½ teaspoon of the oregano, and 1 tablespoon of the olive oil.

When the dough is ready, grease a 10-inch (25 cm) round baking pan with olive oil. Place the dough in the middle of the pan and gently stretch it to fill the pan. Spread the onion-tomato mixture over the dough, followed by the bread crumb topping, the pecorino, and the remaining ½ teaspoon oregano. Drizzle the remaining 1 tablespoon olive oil over everything. Cover the pan with plastic wrap or a clean kitchen towel and let rise in a warm, draft-free place until puffed and pillowy, about 1 hour.

About 15 minutes before the pizza is done rising, preheat the oven to 350°F (180°C).

Remove the plastic wrap or kitchen towel and bake the pizza until the crust is crispy on the bottom and the topping has browned, about 30 minutes.

Let cool for at least 15 minutes before cutting into wedges to serve.

NOTE: Reheat any leftover sfincione in a warm oven before serving.

BREAD CRUMBS

BREAD IS SO SACRED IN SICILIAN FOOD CULTURE THAT NO
waste is allowed, therefore bread crumbs are an essential
ingredient, showing up as a breading on fish and meat cutlets,
as a filling for vegetables, even on pastas and pizzas. Bread
crumbs can also be used instead of flour to coat a pan, which
will give a lovely crunch to whatever crust or cake you are
baking. Though you can purchase bread crumbs at any bakery
in Sicily, many households have a machine that grinds stale
bread into crumbs. Most importantly, these crumbs should
be dry and unseasoned. In recipes such as Bucatini with
Cauliflower, Pine Nuts, and Raisins (page 103) or Spaghetti with
Anchovies and Toasted Bread Crumbs (page 110), they are used
as a topping instead of cheese, while sfincione, the most popular
pizza made in the area around Palermo (see Palermitan Pizza,
page 242), is topped with tomato sauce, lots of onions, and
plenty of bread crumbs.

FOCACCIA WITH BLACK OLIVES AND ROSEMARY

focaccia con olive nere e rosmarino

SERVES 8 TO 10

FOR THE DOUGH

1 tablespoon active dry yeast

½ teaspoon sugar

1½ cups (360 ml) lukewarm water

6¼ cups (1 kg) semolina flour

1 tablespoon fine sea salt

1 cup (240 ml) olive oil, plus more for the bowl, pan, and hands

1 cup (240 ml) white wine

FOR THE TOPPING

¾ cup (100 g) black olives, pitted

Leaves from 2 sprigs of fresh rosemary

Big pinch of flaky sea salt

Olive oil, for drizzling

A combination of wine, olive oil, and water imparts a great deal of fluffiness and moisture to this classic bread. Black olives and rosemary is one favorite topping, but this is equally good with only sea salt on top or with a more involved topping of thinly sliced onion or other vegetables—every home cook will have their own slightly different and very personal variation.

MAKE THE DOUGH: In a small bowl, mix together the yeast, sugar, and 2 tablespoons of the water. Set aside at room temperature until creamy, about 5 minutes. If the yeast doesn't bubble at all, throw it out and start over with new yeast.

In a large bowl, combine the semolina, fine salt, and yeast mixture. Add about half of the remaining water and mix with your hands. Mix in the olive oil and wine until incorporated, then add enough of the remaining water to make a shaggy dough. Turn the dough out onto a work surface and knead until smooth but still quite sticky, about 8 minutes. Shape the dough into a ball and transfer to a large oiled bowl. Cover the bowl with a clean kitchen towel and let the dough rise in a warm, draft-free place until doubled in size, about 1 hour.

Preheat the oven to 400°F (200°C). Oil an 18-by-13-inch (46 by 33 cm) sheet pan.

With oiled hands, press and stretch the dough to fill the prepared pan, adding more olive oil as needed to keep the dough from sticking. Let rise for another 10 minutes.

Top the dough: Pat the dough with your fingertips to make dimples all over it. Scatter the olives on top, sprinkle with rosemary and flaky salt, and drizzle with olive oil.

Bake until golden, about 30 minutes. Let cool slightly before cutting into squares.

FOCACCIA FROM MESSINA WITH ESCAROLE AND TOMATOES

focaccia messinese con scarola e pomodori

FOR THE DOUGH

2 teaspoons active dry yeast

½ teaspoon sugar

1 cup (240 ml) lukewarm water

1⅔ cups (200 g) all-purpose flour, plus more for dusting

1¼ cups (200 g) semolina flour

3 tablespoons olive oil, plus more for the pan and hands

1 teaspoon fine sea salt

FOR THE TOPPINGS

½ head escarole

2 tablespoons olive oil

Fine sea salt and freshly ground black pepper

2 large tomatoes or 1 pint cherry tomatoes

15 to 20 oil-packed anchovy fillets

7 ounces (200 g) tuma, primo sale, or provola cheese, sliced

The dough for this Messinese specialty is made with equal parts semolina and all-purpose flours, and that less intense reliance on semolina may be explained by the proximity of Messina to the mainland. The combination of fresh escarole and juicy tomatoes with the salty anchovies and cheese is superb. A thoughtful nonna would make sure to use a generous amount of each ingredient, so that every square of focaccia includes at least a couple of anchovies and a good hunk of cheese. Tuma and primo sale are the cheeses most often used here, but provolone or another sturdy cheese that doesn't melt too much can also work.

MAKE THE DOUGH: In a small bowl, mix together the yeast, sugar, and 2 tablespoons of the water. Set aside at room temperature until creamy, about 5 minutes. If the yeast doesn't bubble at all, throw it out and start over with new yeast.

In a large bowl, combine the all-purpose flour, semolina flour, olive oil, salt, yeast mixture, and the remaining water. Mix until a shaggy dough forms. Turn it out onto a floured work surface and knead until soft and smooth, about 10 minutes. Cover with a clean kitchen towel and let rest for 10 minutes.

Oil an 18-by-13-inch (46 by 33 cm) sheet pan and, with oiled hands, press and stretch the dough into a thin layer to fill the pan, adding more olive oil as needed to keep the dough from sticking. Cover the pan with plastic wrap and let rise in a warm place for about 1 hour.

Meanwhile, prepare the toppings: Clean the escarole and dry it well. Tear it into bite-size pieces, toss with the olive oil, and season with salt and pepper. If using large tomatoes, peel and chop them, letting them drain in a colander if they are very juicy. If using cherry tomatoes, cut them in half.

After the dough has risen, preheat the oven to 350°F (180°C).

Arrange the anchovies and cheese evenly over the dough. Top evenly with the dressed escarole and the tomatoes.

Bake until the edges are golden brown, about 35 minutes. Remove from the oven and let cool for 10 minutes before cutting into squares. Serve warm or at room temperature.

CHRISTMAS SFOGLIO FROM RAGUSA

sfoglio di natale di ragusa

SERVES 6 TO 8

1 teaspoon active dry yeast

¼ teaspoon sugar

½ cup (120 ml) lukewarm water, plus more as needed

1½ cups (240 g) semolina flour, plus more for dusting

Pinch of fine sea salt

6 tablespoons (90 g) lard, at room temperature

14 ounces (400 g) whole-milk ricotta cheese, well drained

14 ounces (400 g) uncooked Italian sausage, bulk (or casings removed if links)

1 large egg, lightly beaten

Made as a special treat at Christmastime in Ragusa, this dish features a puff pastry–like dough layered with lard and filled with sausage and ricotta. A similar dough is used to make a sweet ricotta-filled pastry called la raviola in Caltanissetta. Like brioche and calzone, this flaky pastry is a local example of how haute-cuisine techniques can be mixed with rustic ingredients. A wedge of sfoglio with a salad of bitter greens or the Fennel-Orange Salad with Black Olives (page 194) makes a perfect lunch.

IN A SMALL bowl, mix together the yeast, sugar, and 2 tablespoons of the water. Set aside at room temperature until creamy, about 5 minutes. If the yeast doesn't bubble at all, throw it out and start over with new yeast.

In a large bowl, combine the semolina, the salt, 1 tablespoon of the lard, the yeast mixture, and the remaining water. Turn it out onto a floured work surface and knead until smooth, about 5 minutes. If the dough is having trouble coming together, drizzle in another tablespoon of water and continue to knead. Shape the dough into a ball, transfer to a bowl, cover, and let rise in a warm place for 2 hours.

On a lightly floured surface, use a rolling pin to roll out the dough into a very thin 24-inch (61 cm) round. Brush a thin layer of lard all over the surface of the dough. Start rolling about 1 inch (2.5 cm) of the dough up from the bottom and brush the folded section with lard. Continue to roll up, brushing each folded section with lard, until you have a long, flat, narrow snake shape. Then, starting at one end, coil up the snake into a snug pinwheel.

Line a baking sheet with parchment paper. Using a sharp knife, cut the pinwheel horizontally in half to make 2 thinner pinwheels. Roll out each pinwheel into a 12-inch (30 cm) round. Place one of the rounds on the prepared baking sheet. Crumble the ricotta and sausage evenly over the dough, leaving a border all around free. Place the other round of dough on top and press the edges to seal. Cover with a towel and let rest in a warm place for 1 hour.

Preheat the oven to 350°F (180°C). Brush the beaten egg over the top of the dough.

Bake the pastry until golden and crisp, 35 to 45 minutes. Remove from the oven and let rest for 15 minutes before cutting into wedges. Serve warm.

NOTE: Leftover sfoglio can be reheated in a low oven until warm.

DESSERTS

dolci

Sicilians have a deep and abiding sweet tooth, one that they share with people in many countries of the southern Mediterranean and North Africa. Any special occasion—wedding, baptism, patron saint festival, other public holiday—is a good excuse to celebrate with a huge amount of food and an array of special cookies and cakes.

Sicily's long history of conquest and religious ritual has created a complex, multilayered culture. You can see this play out in many ways, but especially in the world of pastry, where all Sicilian sweets have a specific story, shape, season, ritual, and meaning. Take, for example, cudduredde, a ring-shaped pastry that is a descendent of the ancient Greek kollura and still appears on the altars celebrating Saint Joseph and in the processions for Saint Paul in Chiaramonte. Then look at the Latin mustaceus, a cookie mentioned by Cato and Apicius made of rye flour, anise, cumin, and cheese that becomes a pastry called mustazzolu made in several small villages around central Sicily. Cuccia, a ritual dish of wheat berries covered in ricotta cream, belonged to the ancient cult of Demeter, the Greek goddess of wheat, but since Christian times has been made to celebrate Saint Lucy, the patron saint of light and sight. Again and again, paganism and Christianity overlap in Sicily and blend into unique and fascinating stories about food and pastry.

Sweetened ricotta, honey, candied fruits, lemon, sesame seeds, almonds, pistachios . . . these are the ingredients that are most often found in Sicilian pastries. It is hard to trace the precise origin of each ingredient, but we know that honey was definitely used by the Greeks, who also introduced almonds and olive trees to Sicily, while sugarcane has most likely been grown since the time of the Roman Empire. Different shapes of sweet and savory empanadas were inherited from centuries of Spanish rule. At the end of the nineteenth century, several families of pastry chefs arrived from Switzerland and established shops in Palermo and Catania. Known as pasticceria svizzera, this type of refined pastry featuring chocolate, butter, and cream can now be found in many shops all over the island.

Cities were central to the development of the art of confectionery. As the capital, Palermo was home to the largest number of aristocratic palaces and the richest churches and monasteries on the island, so there was always a call for elaborate sweets and desserts, such as cassata, the ricotta-filled cake decorated with a baroque arrangement of colorful candied fruits (see Sicilian Cake with Ricotta Cream and Marzipan, page 300). In the island's remote villages, you were more likely to find sweetened fritters or rustic cookies that were tied to a certain feast day or ritual.

Another vital chapter in the intricate history of Sicilian sweets takes place in the many convents scattered around the island. Until the mid-1800s, Sicilian nuns, many of whom came from wealthy families, specialized in elaborate sweets that were made as gifts for the bishops and aristocrats who supported the convents. Strangely enough, many of those sweets have very erotic names, such as Breasts of the Virgin (small round iced pastries filled with candied squash), Ass of the Chancellor (a shell-shaped sandwich of marzipan filled with cream), and Triumph of Gluttony (a layered cake made of marzipan, sponge cake, and candied fruits). The convents were also responsible for many other iconic treats, including highly realistic fruits made of marzipan (made by the nuns of the Martorana church in Palermo); a sweet couscous from the convent of Santo Spirito in Agrigento; cookies stuffed with candied squash from Palma di Montechiaro; and the olivette di Sant'Agata, little green marzipan olives made in Catania. After the unification of Italy and the subsequent suppression of the convents, nuns continued to sell their pastries to the public as a way to support themselves. Slowly, over the last hundred years, most of those traditional recipes have passed into the hands of pastry chefs who are now producing them to be sold in their stores.

WATERMELON PUDDING

gelo di mellone

SERVES 8

One 7-pound (3.15 kg) piece watermelon

½ cup (70 g) cornstarch

¾ to 1 cup (150 to 200 g) sugar, depending on the sweetness of the melon

Fresh jasmine blossoms, bittersweet chocolate shavings, candied squash, or chopped pistachios, for garnish

Sicilians understand and appreciate the difference between opaque, velvety puddings and transparent, wobbly gelatins. Despite its misleading name, gelo di mellone is one of many dolci al cucchiaio that, like the Sicilian recipes for lemon curd and coffee jelly, is thickened with either cornstarch or wheat starch. Typically prepared for the Feast of Saint Rosalia in mid-July in Palermo and western Sicily, watermelon pudding is often decorated with white jasmine flowers, which are in bloom at the same time. Use the sweetest, most full-flavored melon you can find for this treat.

CUT OFF AND discard the rind from the watermelon. Coarsely chop the watermelon into chunks. In a blender, puree enough chopped watermelon to yield 6 cups (1.5 L) puree.

Strain the watermelon puree through a fine-mesh sieve into a medium saucepan. Whisk in the cornstarch and sugar and bring to a boil, whisking constantly to prevent lumps. When the mixture comes to a boil, cook for 1 minute, then remove from the heat.

Pour the mixture into one large dish or small bowls or glasses. Let cool, then refrigerate until well chilled. Garnish as desired before serving.

NOTE: The pudding can be made up to 2 days ahead and refrigerated, wrapped well in plastic wrap.

GELATO IN SICILY

FOR CENTURIES, MEN HARVESTED THE WINTER SNOW THAT gathered on Mount Etna or in the Madonie Mountains and stored it in naturally insulated caves called fosse. In summer, they would dig out the ice, pack it tightly in straw and salt, and load it up on donkeys to travel around the island, providing relief during the hottest months of the year, first in the form of iced drinks and later with more elaborate sorbets, granitas, and gelatos.

The word *sciroppo* (a thick, sweet syrup based on fruit juice) comes from the Arabic root *sh-r-b*, meaning "to drink," and appears throughout Europe in the fourteenth century. A bit later, the Persian word *sharbat* appears, then the Turkish and later Ottoman *serbet*, which around the sixteenth century became *sorbet* or *sorbetto*, reflecting the Safavid and Ottoman custom of drinking fruit juices sweetened with sugar and often cooled with ice. Those cold drinks were the first steps in developing sorbetto, granita, and cremolada, frozen concoctions with differing textures according to the quantity of sugar added—the more sugary the syrup, the softer it remains as it freezes. Granita has fluffy ice shards, while sorbetto and cremolada are smoother and creamier.

Up until the 1950s, fruit sorbets were reserved for fancy, upscale banquets as a palate cleanser during a meal, while regular Sicilians cooled off with shaved ice drizzled with syrup, sold from a street cart. Now, when the weather starts warming up, crowds of all ages, from seniors to teenagers, swarm like bees during the afternoon passeggiata to enjoy gelato or sorbets in cones or scooped into a fluffy brioche.

Beyond gelato, sorbet, and granita, there is a whole world of masterful Sicilian iced desserts, for example: the cassata gelato, an old-fashioned and beautiful layered ice cream that combines vanilla, pistachios, and Chantilly cream surrounded by a case of sponge cake, all frozen so what you eat is a colorful slice of multiple flavors. The *pezzi duri* ("hard pieces"), based on water, not cream, are famous in Palermo, while spumone, a layered dome of ice cream surrounding a heart of zabaione that is served in slices, is typical in the city of Acireale on the east coast.

ALMOND GRANITA

granita alle mandorle

MAKES ABOUT 4 CUPS (1 L)

1 cup (150 g) almonds, blanched and peeled

¾ cup plus ⅓ cup (220 g) sugar

2⅔ cups (640 ml) water

2 tablespoons honey

Freshly ground almonds lend a velvety richness to this completely dairy-free dessert. When you order granita in a café, it often comes with a round brioche roll that can be torn and dunked into the melting icy treat.

IN A FOOD processor, combine the almonds and ¾ cup (150 g) of the sugar and pulse until very finely ground.

Transfer the almond paste to a saucepan. Add the water and cook over medium-low heat, stirring occasionally, until the sugar has dissolved, about 5 minutes. Let sit for about 2 hours for the mixture to infuse.

If you want a very smooth granita, press the mixture through a sieve. If you don't mind a bit of texture, you can leave it as is.

Add the honey and remaining ⅓ cup (70 g) sugar to the almond mixture, stirring until dissolved.

Pour the mixture into a large metal baking pan and freeze, stirring with a fork every 30 minutes, until the mixture is firm but not frozen hard, 3 to 4 hours.

Before serving, scrape the granita with a fork to lighten the texture. (Alternatively, the mixture can be frozen in an ice cream maker, which will produce a more sorbet-like texture.)

NOTE: Granita can be made up to 1 day ahead.

LEMON GRANITA

granita di limone

MAKES ABOUT 4 CUPS (1 L)

8 lemons

2 cups (480 ml) water

1¼ cups (250 g) sugar

Lemon granita is a classic of Sicilian summer, and when the heat waves of July and August hit, you see granita everywhere. Once upon a time, all granita was made by hand, which required stirring and scraping the concoction every half hour to produce fluffy ice crystals, but now bars in Sicily serve it from machines made of clear plexiglass so you can watch as the sweet, refreshing slush is constantly stirred. When making homemade granita, it is crucial to allow the whole mixture to freeze gradually and evenly. This still means stirring frequently while it starts freezing at the edges of the container.

The most popular lemons in Sicily are the Interdonato from Messina (the name comes from Giovanni Interdonato, a colonel in the Garibaldi army) and the Femminello from Siracusa, considered to be the juiciest lemon in the world.

USING A VEGETABLE peeler or a small sharp knife, carefully peel the zest from the lemons in strips, avoiding any spongy white pith. In a bowl, combine the strips of zest and the water and allow to infuse overnight.

Juice enough of the peeled lemons to make 1 cup (240 ml) juice. Refrigerate until ready to use.

The next day, remove the lemon zests from the water. Add the sugar to the water and stir until dissolved. Stir in the lemon juice.

Pour the mixture into a large metal baking pan and freeze, stirring with a fork every 30 minutes, until the mixture is firm but not frozen hard, 3 to 4 hours.

Before serving, scrape the granita with a fork to lighten the texture. (Alternatively, the mixture can be frozen in an ice cream maker, which will produce a more sorbet-like texture.)

NOTE: Granita can be made up to 1 day ahead.

QUINCE POACHED IN RED WINE

melecotogne al vino

SERVES 4

2 quinces

2 cups (480 ml) red wine

1 small cinnamon stick or a
pinch of ground cinnamon

2 whole cloves

2 bay leaves

3 strips of orange zest
(use a vegetable peeler)

¼ cup (50 g) sugar

Vanilla gelato (optional), for
serving

Although it looks like a cross between an apple and a pear,
a quince is too hard and tart to eat raw and must be cooked
with some sort of liquid, usually water or wine, and lots of
sugar. Cotognata, a thick quince paste that is very similar
to Spanish membrillo, is the most common way the fruit is
eaten in Sicily, where the paste is poured into lovely ceramic
molds that come in the shapes of fish, fruits, and decorative
arabesques. It is enjoyed simply as a sweet on its own, not as
an accompaniment to cheese, as it is in Spain. Poaching quince
and serving it with gelato is another, simpler way of enjoying
this very special fruit.

PREHEAT THE OVEN to 350°F (180°C).

Peel and core the quinces, then cut each one into 4 wedges.
Place the wedges in a deep baking dish just large enough to hold
them snugly. Pour in the wine—it should go a bit more than
halfway up the sides of the fruit—and add the cinnamon, cloves,
bay leaves, and orange zest. Sprinkle the sugar over everything.

Bake until the quince is soft all the way through when poked
with a fork, 35 to 45 minutes.

Use a slotted spoon to carefully transfer the poached quince to
a plate. Set aside.

Strain the cooking liquid from the baking dish in a fine-mesh
sieve set over a small saucepan. Bring the liquid to a boil and cook
until reduced and syrupy, 5 to 8 minutes.

Serve the poached quince drizzled with the syrup and topped
with a big scoop of vanilla gelato, if desired.

HONEY

HONEY IS USED NOT ONLY IN SICILIAN SWEETS—SUCH AS pignoccata (opposite) and versions of sfince di San Giuseppe (see page 295)—but also in savory dishes such as fried cardoons. Due to genetic crossing, pesticides, and climate change, today's bees are facing a very difficult time. Thirty years ago, agronomist and scholar Carlo Amodeo began rescuing the native Sicilian black bee, which has survived in Sicily for millennia with its genes intact. It has an extraordinary resilience to pests as well as changing climate conditions. Amodeo has installed new colonies in western Sicily and has a team of beekeepers working to protect the bees and harvest their honey. Today, honeys are available from almond blossom, loquat, sulla, and orange blossom as well as the array of wildflowers available all year round in Sicily.

FRIED DOUGH BALLS WITH HONEY

pignoccata

2¼ cups (300 g) all-purpose flour

⅓ cup (80 g) sugar

5 tablespoons (70 g) unsalted butter, at room temperature, cut into cubes

Finely grated zest of 1 lemon

3 large eggs

Pinch of fine sea salt

Vegetable oil, for frying

½ cup plus 1 tablespoon (200 g) honey

Rainbow sprinkles (optional)

Almonds (optional)

Pizzicata, pignoccata, pignolata . . . these are all names for a dish of little fried dough balls coated in honey and piled up in the shape of a *pigna* ("pine cone"). With its many seeds, the pine cone is naturally symbolic, calling to mind a prosperous future or a bountiful harvest, and pignoccata is traditionally made for Carnival. As with so many Sicilian dishes, variations abound. In Messina, for instance, pignoccata is usually baked instead of fried and presented with half of the dough balls covered in chocolate and half in a lemony white icing. This is the kind of sweet you put out after dinner, encouraging everyone to linger at the table while they pluck another piece from the pile, talking late into the evening.

IN A STAND mixer fitted with a paddle, beat together the flour, sugar, butter, lemon zest, eggs, and salt until a thick, smooth dough forms. Cover the bowl with plastic wrap or a clean kitchen towel and let rest for 30 minutes.

After the dough has rested, pinch off a piece and roll it into a long rope ½ inch (1.25 cm) thick. Cut the rope crosswise into ¾-inch (2 cm) lengths. If you like, lightly roll each piece into a ball. Repeat with the rest of the dough.

Pour 2 inches (5 cm) of vegetable oil into a large heavy saucepan and heat over medium-high heat until it is hot enough to fry in (see Deep-Frying, page 30). Line a plate with paper towels.

Once the oil heats up, deep-fry the dough pieces, working in batches to avoid crowding the pan, until they turn light golden brown, about 2 minutes, then drain on the paper towels.

Warm the honey in a spouted glass measuring cup in a small saucepan of water until it is runny.

Place the pignoccata balls in a large bowl, drizzle in the warmed honey, and toss until coated and glossy. Arrange on a serving platter, mounding the balls in the shape of a pine cone or pyramid. Scatter the rainbow sprinkles and almonds on top, if using.

NOTES

- The pignoccata can be fried, cooled, and stored in an airtight container up to 1 day ahead. Toss with honey just before serving.

- The assembled pignoccata can be made up to 3 hours in advance and kept, loosely covered in plastic wrap, at room temperature.

ROLLED FIG COOKIES

buccellati

MAKES ABOUT 20 COOKIES

FOR THE DOUGH

4 tablespoons (60 g) lard or unsalted butter, at room temperature

¼ cup (50 g) granulated sugar

1 large egg

1 tablespoon whole milk

¼ teaspoon vanilla extract

2 cups (240 g) all-purpose flour

½ teaspoon baking powder

FOR THE FILLING

½ cup (50 g) walnuts, toasted and chopped

½ cup (65 g) almonds, toasted and chopped

¼ cup (35 g) pistachios, toasted and chopped

5 ounces (150 g) dried figs, very finely chopped

⅓ cup (100 g) orange or tangerine marmalade

⅔ cup (160 ml) mosto cotto (see Resources, page 310) or ¼ cup (60 ml) molasses plus enough white wine to make ⅔ cup

FOR DECORATION

1 cup (120 g) powdered sugar

Juice of 1 lemon

Rainbow sprinkles

Buccellati, cookies stuffed with dried fruits and nuts, are the most traditional Sicilian Christmas sweet and are made all over the island, in different shapes and with all kinds of variations. In large towns, you might find imposing versions shaped like a big doughnut, while elsewhere the buccellati are much smaller and fan shaped. They are often iced and festively decorated with colorful sprinkles. In many versions the preparation of buccellati requires the use of mosto cotto, a reduced grape must that has been flavored with cinnamon, cloves, carob, and orange zest. It is sometimes called vino cotto, but technically it is made with *mosto* ("must," or unfermented grape juice), not wine. For centuries in Sicily, mosto cotto was used as a substitute for sugar, and in country villages, it has often been used as a syrup to treat coughs and colds.

MAKE THE DOUGH: In a stand mixer fitted with a paddle, beat the lard and granulated sugar until fluffy and lightened in color, about 3 minutes. Add the egg, milk, and vanilla and mix until well combined. Add the flour and baking powder and mix until a soft, smooth dough forms. Wrap the dough in plastic wrap and refrigerate for at least 30 minutes.

Make the filling: In a food processor, pulse the walnuts, almonds, and pistachios until finely ground. Transfer to a large bowl and add the dried figs, marmalade, and mosto cotto. Mix well. Pour the filling mixture into a large saucepan and cook over medium-low heat, stirring constantly, until the figs soften and the mixture thickens, 3 to 5 minutes. Return the filling to the bowl and let cool completely.

Preheat the oven to 350°F (180°C). Line two baking sheets with parchment paper.

Divide the chilled dough into 4 equal portions. Working with 1 portion at a time, roll out the dough into a 3-by-15-inch (7 by 38 cm) rectangle about ⅛ inch (3 mm) thick. Transfer the cooled fig filling to a pastry bag fitted with a #12 (⅓-inch/1 cm) plain tip. (Alternatively, just use a small spoon.) With a long side of the dough rectangle facing you, pipe (or spoon) a line of filling about two fingers' distance from the dough's top edge along the length of the rectangle. Fold the bottom of the dough up over the filling and then fold the top down to enclose the filling. Turn the log seam-side down and press gently to seal and flatten a bit. Repeat with the remaining dough and filling.

recipe continues

Using a small knife or scissors, cut slits about every ¾ inch (19 mm) down the log and about ⅓ of the way into the log. Cut each log into 3-inch (7 cm) segments and gently pull apart the slits to open each cookie into a fan shape. Place the cookies on the prepared baking sheets.

Bake until the cookies are golden, about 20 minutes. Let cool on the baking sheets.

While the cookies cool, prepare the decorations: In a small bowl, stir together the powdered sugar and enough lemon juice to achieve a smooth but dippable consistency. When the cookies are completely cool, dip the tops into the icing and decorate with rainbow sprinkles.

NOTE: The cookies can be stored in an airtight container for up to 1 week.

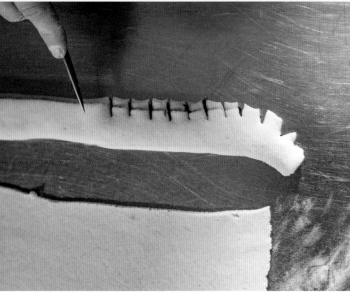

RICOTTA-FILLED TURNOVERS

cassatelle di ricotta

MAKES ABOUT 20
TURNOVERS

7 tablespoons (105 ml)
white wine

3 tablespoons olive oil

2 cups (320 g) semolina flour,
plus more for dusting

Pinch of fine sea salt

1 cup (250 g) whole-milk
ricotta cheese, preferably
sheep's milk, well drained

3 tablespoons granulated
sugar

½ teaspoon ground
cinnamon, plus more
(optional) for garnish

Vegetable oil, for frying

Powdered sugar, for garnish

EQUIPMENT
Pasta machine

Cassatelle are typical in the Trapani area, where locals eat them instead of cornetti (Italian croissants, often filled with jam or marmalade) while sipping their morning coffee. Stuffed with ricotta and dusted with cinnamon and powdered sugar, these half-moon pastries can be fried or baked, but most consider the fried ones to be far more delicious.

IN A SMALL saucepan, heat the wine and olive oil over medium heat until just warm (not hot). Remove from the heat and set aside.

Mound the semolina on a clean work surface and make a well in the center. Add the salt and the wine-oil mixture to the well and, with a fork, carefully mix them into the flour. Knead the dough with your hands until smooth and elastic, about 5 minutes.

In a separate small bowl, stir together the ricotta, granulated sugar, and cinnamon. Set aside.

Cut the dough into quarters, keeping the remaining dough wrapped as you work.

Set a pasta machine to the thickest setting. Run a piece of dough through the machine about five times at this setting, folding the dough in half each time before rolling it again. When the dough is very even, move the dial to the next thinner setting and roll it through two or three times more, folding it each time, until it is about 1/16 inch (2 mm) thick.

Lay the dough on a floured work surface and cut out rounds with a 4-inch (10 cm) round cookie cutter. Place a spoonful of the ricotta mixture just off-center on one of the dough rounds, then moisten the edges of the dough with water and fold over. Pinch firmly to seal. Repeat with the remaining dough and filling, rerolling the scraps as needed.

Pour 2 inches (5 cm) of vegetable oil into a large heavy-bottomed pot and heat over medium-high heat until it is hot enough to fry in (see Deep-Frying, page 30). Line a large sheet pan with paper towels.

Once the oil is ready, slip a few cassatelle into the hot oil, taking care to not crowd the pan, and fry, flipping occasionally, until deep golden, about 3 minutes. With a slotted spoon or skimmer, transfer to the paper towels to drain. Repeat with the remaining cassatelle.

Sprinkle powdered sugar and cinnamon, if using, over the cassatelle and serve warm.

NOTE: Cassatelle taste best when freshly fried, but leftover pastries can be reheated in a 350°F (180°C) oven until warm and crisp, 8 to 10 minutes.

KNOTTED LEMON COOKIES

taralli

MAKES ABOUT 4 DOZEN
COOKIES

4 cups (480 g) all-purpose
flour, plus more for dusting

½ cup (100 g) granulated
sugar

½ cup (120 g) lard

1½ tablespoons powdered
ammonium carbonate (also
called baker's ammonia or
hartshorn)

Finely grated zest of 1 lemon,
plus the juice of 1 to 2 lemons

Pinch of fine sea salt

2 large eggs

⅔ cup (160 ml) whole milk,
lukewarm

2 cups (240 g) powdered
sugar

Grated orange zest (optional),
for garnish

Sweet Sicilian taralli are totally different from the better-known savory taralli from Puglia. Long ago, these knotted cookies glazed with a simple lemony icing were made to commemorate All Souls' Day on November 2, but now they can be found year-round. Their unique consistency—a very light crispness—comes from ammonium carbonate, a common leavener for Sicilian cookies. (Don't worry—its strong odor dissipates completely during baking.) These sweet little biscuits are just the thing to accompany a midafternoon espresso or cup of tea.

IN A BOWL, whisk together the flour and granulated sugar. With your hands, work in the lard, ammonium carbonate, lemon zest, and salt. Make a well in the center and start working in the eggs, and then the milk, bit by bit, with your hands, just until the mixture comes together into a very soft dough (you may not need to use all the milk). Knead the dough vigorously; it is done when the dough pulls off your fingers easily but is still quite sticky.

Preheat the oven to 350°F (180°C). Line two baking sheets with parchment paper.

On a lightly floured surface, roll a piece of dough into a rope ½ inch (1.25 cm) thick. Cut it crosswise into 5-inch (12.5 cm) lengths. Form a loop with a length of dough and then insert one end through the center of the loop to form a knot. Place on a prepared baking sheet. Repeat with the remaining dough and baking sheet.

Bake until golden brown, about 20 minutes.

Meanwhile, in a small bowl, mix the powdered sugar and enough lemon juice to achieve a thin icing. Dip the top of each cookie in the icing and transfer to a rack to cool. Sprinkle with orange zest, if using.

NOTE: The cookies can be stored for up to 1 week in an airtight container.

QUEEN'S COOKIES
biscotti regina

MAKES ABOUT 5 DOZEN
COOKIES

4½ cups (540 g) all-purpose
flour

1 cup (200 g) sugar

Pinch of fine sea salt

1 large egg

4 egg yolks

1¾ sticks (7 ounces/200 g)
butter, at cool room
temperature, cut into pieces

Whole milk, as needed

1 cup (160 g) sesame seeds

Some bakeries, besides selling bread and some snacks such as calzone and arancine, will sell a few different types of simple cookies, much plainer than the sweets sold in pastry shops. The most popular cookie found in any good bakery in Sicily, especially around Palermo, is biscotti regina. Also known as reginelle, these crunchy sesame seed–covered treats are delightful dipped into a coffee or a glass of sweet Marsala wine.

IN A STAND mixer fitted with a paddle (or in a large bowl with a handheld mixer), beat together the flour, sugar, salt, whole egg, egg yolks, and butter until the dough just comes together. Do not overwork. Add a splash of milk if the dough is too dry.

Preheat the oven to 350°F (180°C). Line two baking sheets with parchment paper.

Fill one bowl with cold water and another with the sesame seeds. Divide the dough into quarters. Roll one quarter into a long rope 1 inch (2.5 cm) thick. Cut the rope into 2-inch (5 cm) lengths. Working in batches, quickly dip several pieces of dough in the water, then in the sesame seeds to coat. Repeat with the remaining dough and sesame seeds.

Arrange the pieces on the prepared baking sheets and bake until golden brown, 20 to 30 minutes. Transfer to a rack to cool.

NOTE: The cookies can be stored for up to 1 week in an airtight container.

CANNOLI WITH RICOTTA CREAM
cannoli con crema di ricotta

MAKES 20 TO 30 CANNOLI

FOR THE RICOTTA

1 pound (450 g) whole-milk ricotta cheese

FOR THE SHELLS

2 cups (240 g) all-purpose flour, plus more for dusting

1 tablespoon granulated sugar

2½ teaspoons unsweetened cocoa powder

Pinch of fine sea salt

1½ tablespoons lard or unsalted butter, at room temperature

1½ tablespoons dry Marsala wine

1 teaspoon red or white wine vinegar

1 large egg, beaten

1 to 2 tablespoons water, as needed

Vegetable oil, for frying

FOR THE FILLING AND ASSEMBLY

½ to ¾ cup (60 to 90 g) powdered sugar, plus more for dusting

Chopped pistachios, mini chocolate chips, and/or candied orange peel, for garnish

EQUIPMENT

¾-inch-diameter (2 cm) cannoli molds (see Resources, page 310)

Pasta machine

"Leave the gun. Take the cannoli," says Pete Clemenza after the murder of Don Vito Corleone's driver in *The Godfather*. Such is the importance of a good cannolo to Sicilians! Every pastry shop sells cannoli, but, as any Sicilian knows, cannoli need to be "espresso"—filled on the spot—otherwise the shells become soggy. A cannolo's surface is covered in bumps and bubbles produced by a small amount of wine and vinegar in the dough. The most renowned cannoli come from areas celebrated for the quality of their ricotta, such as Piana degli Albanesi, south of Palermo. (In addition to its delicious cow's-milk ricotta, the town is famous for the fact that many Albanians settled there in the 1600s and have fully retained their language and culture.) Tubular cannoli molds are most often made of metal (though you will sometimes see them made of wooden dowels). Look for ones that are about ¾ inch (2 cm) in diameter.

PREPARE THE RICOTTA: A couple of days before you'd like to make the cannoli, drain the ricotta: Transfer the ricotta to a sieve set over a bowl and place in the refrigerator to drain for 1 to 2 days. (It is very important that the ricotta be well drained; otherwise the filling will be runny.)

Make the cannoli shells: In a large bowl, whisk together the flour, granulated sugar, cocoa, and salt. Using your hands, rub in the lard until well distributed. Add the Marsala, vinegar, half of the beaten egg (save the other half for a later step), and 1 tablespoon of the water. Knead until a smooth dough forms; it should be quite stiff. If the dough doesn't come together, mix in the remaining 1 tablespoon water. Shape the dough into a ball, wrap in plastic wrap, and refrigerate for at least 30 minutes.

Cut the dough into quarters, keeping the remaining dough wrapped as you work.

Set a pasta machine to the thickest setting. Run a piece of dough through the machine about five times at this setting, folding the dough in half each time before rolling it again. When the dough is very smooth, move the dial to the next thinner setting and roll it through one time without folding. Continue rolling the dough without folding it, once on each setting, until the dough is about ¹⁄₁₆ inch (2 mm) thick. The dough should be very even and silky. Lay the rolled dough sheet on a lightly floured surface. Repeat the rolling process with the rest of the dough.

Use a lightly floured 3½- to 4-inch (9 to 10 cm) round cookie cutter to cut rounds from the dough. Reroll the dough scraps and continue cutting out rounds until you've used up all the dough.

Pour at least 2 inches (5 cm) of vegetable oil into a wide heavy-bottomed pot and heat over medium-high heat until it is hot enough to fry in (see Deep-Frying, page 30). Line a large plate with paper towels.

Meanwhile, work with about 4 molds at a time and keep the remaining dough covered while you work. Wrap a dough round around a cannoli mold, keeping it loose and leaving a little space between the dough and the mold. (Wrapping it loosely will make it easier to remove after frying.) Dab the edge of the dough with some of the reserved beaten egg and press to seal.

Once the oil is ready, slip a few of the wrapped cannoli molds into the hot oil, working in batches to avoid crowding the pan, and fry until golden, bubbly, and crisp, 1 to 2 minutes. Use tongs to gently pick up the fried shells and molds and transfer to the paper towels to drain. Once they're cool enough to handle, slip the shells off the molds. Repeat with the remaining dough rounds and molds.

Make the filling: In a bowl, combine the drained ricotta and ½ cup (60 g) of the powdered sugar. Whisk together until very smooth. Taste and mix in a bit more sugar if you'd like the filling to be sweeter.

Just before serving, assemble the cannoli: Use a piping bag or a tiny spoon to push the filling in at both ends until the shells are completely filled. Garnish by dipping the ends in chopped pistachios or mini chocolate chips, or simply dot with a piece of candied orange peel. Dust with powdered sugar and serve immediately. Filled cannoli are best eaten right away.

NOTE: The unfilled cannoli shells can be stored in an airtight container at room temperature for up to 1 month.

CHOCOLATE

WHEN ONE THINKS OF MODICA, ONE OF THE BAROQUE GEMS
of southeast Sicily, chocolate is one of the first things to come to
mind. In the last three decades, chocolate has become a sign
of identity for the whole city, thanks in large part to Franco Ruta,
the chocolatier who owned the Antica Dolceria Bonajuto. (See
Resources, page 310, for where to buy Bonajuto chocolates.)
At a time when no one outside Ragusa knew of the existence
of cioccolato modicano, Ruta devoted his life to rediscovering
and promoting this very special chocolate that dates back
hundreds of years. In the sixteenth and seventeenth centuries,
conquistadores began returning from South America and
introduced chocolate to Europe, where it quickly became a
passion for European aristocrats. At that time, Spain ruled all
of Sicily, but Modica actually remained under Spanish control
for nearly one hundred years longer than the rest of the island,
which may explain why Modica is the only place on the island
with this lasting chocolate tradition.

Chocolate from Modica has a singular texture—granular and
slightly crunchy. The sandiness is due to its ancient production
technique, which forgoes the last two steps of modern chocolate
making—conching and tempering—which were invented by
Rudolf Lindt in 1879 to create the smooth, melt-in-your-mouth
chocolate familiar to most. Modicana chocolate makers
also season their bars with all sorts of spices, such as vanilla,
cardamom, cinnamon, nutmeg, and tangerine. The bean-to-bar
trend has introduced an even greater array of interesting flavors,
notes, and thoughts of terroir to this ancient style of chocolate.
Chocolate makers from Modica, like many in other countries of
the world, are now buying cacao beans directly from Bolivian or
Peruvian growers and producing single-origin bars.

RICOTTA

IN SICILY, RICOTTA CAN BE MADE FROM EITHER SHEEP'S OR
cow's milk, depending on where you are. Sheep dominate the
interior of the island, and the ricotta there has a strong, slightly
gamy taste and a light, cloudlike texture. The southwest area
around Modica and Ragusa produces mostly cow's-milk ricotta,
which is smoother and milder.

Ricotta, which means "recooked," is technically not a cheese
at all. It is made by taking the whey left over from cheesemaking
and gently reheating it with whole milk and salt until soft curds
form a second time. The curds are scooped into baskets and are
generally eaten fresh. The shepherd could keep these "leftovers,"
which are relatively low in protein, after giving the farmer or
landowner the proper cheese (pecorino in the case of sheep's
milk; caciocavallo in the case of cow's).

Since Sicily produces no cream or butter, ricotta has
become a versatile ingredient that is used to add creaminess to
all kinds of dishes. As a savory ingredient, it can be mixed into
sauces for pasta or coated in bread crumbs and deep-fried as
an appetizer (see Ricotta Fritters, page 29). Or it can be salted
and dried (ricotta salata) or baked slowly at a low temperature
(ricotta infornata), both of which are excellent grated over
pasta. Sweetened ricotta is the best filling for cannoli (page 288),
cassatelle (page 281), and the magnificent cassata (page 300),
as well as many other sweets.

FRIED PUFFS OF SAINT JOSEPH

sfince di san giuseppe

MAKES ABOUT 24 PUFFS

FOR THE SFINCE

1 cup (240 ml) water

5 tablespoons (70 g) unsalted butter, cut into pieces

Fine sea salt

½ teaspoon baking soda

2 cups (240 g) all-purpose flour

6 large eggs, at room temperature

Vegetable oil, for frying

FOR THE GARNISH

1 cup (250 g) whole-milk ricotta cheese

3 tablespoons sugar

24 pieces candied orange peel

Finely chopped pistachios

Saint Joseph is one of the most celebrated saints in all of Italy, and every region in Sicily honors him on March 19, with many towns holding processions and community meals full of special ritual foods. Many of the foods are fried, so much so that Saint Joseph is jokingly called *il santo frittellaro* ("the doughnut saint")! The fried choux-pastry puffs known as sfince are always part of the celebratory spread and are traditionally spread with sweetened ricotta or dipped in honey.

MAKE THE SFINCE: In a saucepan, combine the water, butter, and a pinch of salt and cook over medium heat until the butter melts and the water boils rapidly. Add the baking soda (the mixture will bubble up), then add the flour and stir vigorously until well combined and the mixture pulls away from the sides of the pan, about 30 seconds. Remove from the heat, transfer to the bowl of a stand mixer, and let cool completely.

Using a paddle attachment, add the eggs 1 at a time, beating the mixture until very smooth before adding the next egg. Once all the eggs have been added, beat the mixture until very smooth, about 2 minutes.

Pour 2 inches (5 cm) of vegetable oil into a large heavy-bottomed pot and heat over medium-high heat until it is hot enough to fry in (see Deep-Frying, page 30). Line a large plate with paper towels.

Once the oil is ready, spoon out almond-size pieces of dough and carefully push them off the spoon with your fingers into the hot oil. Fry several at a time, but do not crowd the skillet; the puffs will triple in size and need room to turn as they swell. Cook, turning with a skimmer or tongs, until golden brown on all sides, about 3 minutes. Transfer to the paper towels to drain. Fry the remaining puffs in batches, allowing the oil to heat up again before starting each new batch.

Prepare the garnish: In a small bowl, whisk together the ricotta and sugar. Spread a little ricotta cream over each sfince, top with a piece of candied orange peel, and sprinkle with chopped pistachios. Serve at once.

NOTE: In place of the ricotta cream garnish, the puffs can be drizzled with 1 cup (336 g) warmed honey.

ALMONDS

ALMONDS, WHETHER WHOLE, COARSELY GROUND INTO
almond meal, or made into a fine flour, are vital to the world
of Sicilian confectionery. There are more than 250 varieties of
Prunus dulcis growing around the island, and certain varieties
are used for very specific purposes. For instance, almonds from
Avola in southeast Sicily are particularly prized for their uniform
shape and are used to make confetti—whole almonds covered
in a crunchy sugar coating that are mandatory for any kind of
family celebration.

The bitter almond, *Prunus dulcis* var. *amara*, comes from the
same species as the sweet almond, but while the tree has an
identical aspect, its fruit is unbearably bitter. A very small amount
of cyanide in the nuts produces that bitterness, which is why bitter
almonds are almost impossible to purchase. However, because
they express such a pure almond essence, bitter almonds have
been used in very small amounts for centuries. Today, good-
quality almond extract makes an acceptable substitute.

In Sicily there are slight differences between marzipan and
almond paste (known as *pasta reale*, "royal paste," though the
names are often used interchangeably). Marzipan is usually a
simple, uncooked dough made with almond flour, sugar, water,
and possibly a little glucose or honey. It holds together thanks to
the essential oils from the almonds, but this also means you must
take care not to overknead the dough. This type of marzipan is
used to make the green collar for a cassata (page 300).

Marzipan has made an amazing journey through history. Its
introduction dates back to the time of the Crusades, as it spread
from the Middle East to remote corners of Europe where no
almond tree could possibly grow. Strangely enough, there was
a time when cuisines from the north and south were not so far
apart, and this explains why marzipan cookies are highly prized
not just in Sicily but also in Austria, Denmark, Sweden, and the
United Kingdom.

Pasta reale is made by cooking almond flour and sugar
syrup or glucose together and will hold its shape like Play-Doh.
It most likely got its name because it belonged to the royal
kitchens of the Norman Palace in Palermo. From there pasta reale
moved to the kitchens of the Martorana convent in Palermo.

For Palermitans, frutta di pasta reale is synonymous with frutta di Martorana, wonderful little confections that come shaped like every conceivable type of fruit. They were originally made by the nuns at the Martorana convent. Other treats made from pasta reale include the famous green "olives" made in Catania for the Feast of Saint Agatha and little Easter lambs, which can be molded lying down or sitting on one side and come decorated with realistic-looking wooly curls. Additionally, a third type of almond paste is made from almond flour, sugar, and egg white and gently baked to make popular almond thumbprint cookies.

SICILIAN CAKE WITH RICOTTA CREAM AND MARZIPAN

cassata

SERVES 8 TO 10

FOR THE SPONGE CAKE

Softened butter and flour, for the pan

6 large eggs, at room temperature

¾ cup (150 g) granulated sugar

Finely grated zest of 1 orange

1 cup (120 g) cake flour, sifted

FOR THE MARZIPAN

⅔ cup (100 g) pistachios

1½ cups (150 g) almond flour

¾ cup (90 g) powdered sugar, plus more for dusting

2 tablespoons water

1 teaspoon corn syrup or honey

Green food coloring

FOR ASSEMBLY

2 tablespoons limoncello or Grand Marnier

2 cups (500 g) whole-milk ricotta cheese

⅓ cup (70 g) granulated sugar

FOR DECORATION

1½ cups (180 g) powdered sugar

2 tablespoons fresh lemon juice

Candied fruit (see Resources, page 310)

This sponge cake filled with ricotta cream perfectly illustrates the circuitous path of so many Sicilian pastries that started with a humble ingredient and ended up as an artful confection, in this case decorated with a bright green marzipan belt, glossy white icing, and, most notably, a colorfully baroque decoration of candied fruits. Cassata is an architectural dish, built layer upon layer, so balance is key: A cook must strive to create a cake in which all the flavors are present in each mouthful, with none overpowering another. What helps set a great cassata off from a merely good one is homemade marzipan, which should sing with the rich butteriness of pistachios and almonds. (Fortunately, making marzipan is an easy task.) Traditionally cassata is built in a specific type of sloped pan, which at the bottom has a number (1, 2, 3, etc.) according to the number of kilos one's cassata is going to weigh; however, a deep-dish pie plate will also work. Once the pinnacle of Sicilian Easter desserts, cassata is now eaten all year round.

MAKE THE SPONGE cake: Preheat the oven to 350°F (180°C). Butter and flour a 9-inch (23 cm) springform pan.

In a stand mixer fitted with a whisk, beat the eggs until very light and creamy, about 10 minutes. Add the granulated sugar and orange zest and continue to beat until a ribbon falls slowly from the whisk when lifted, about 5 minutes more. In two or three additions, gently fold in the flour. Pour the batter into the prepared pan and smooth the top.

Bake until a toothpick inserted into the center of the cake comes out clean, 25 to 30 minutes. Let the cake cool completely in the pan on a wire rack.

Meanwhile, make the marzipan: In a food processor, blend the pistachios until very finely ground. Transfer to a large bowl and mix in the almond flour and powdered sugar. Make a well in the center and add the water, corn syrup, and a few drops of food coloring. Mix to form a smooth dough. Dust a work surface with powdered sugar and roll out the dough into a rectangle about 6 by 10 inches (15 by 25 cm) and between ⅛ and ¼ inch (3 and 6 mm) thick. Cut 3 strips that are about 2 inches (5 cm) wide and 10 inches (25 cm) long. Knead any remaining marzipan dough into a ball, wrap it in plastic wrap, and store in the refrigerator for another use.

EQUIPMENT

9-inch (23 cm) springform pan

9-inch (23 cm) cassata pan (see Resources, page 310) or deep-dish pie plate

Assemble the cake: Line a 9-inch (23 cm) cassata pan with plastic wrap. Arrange the marzipan strips along the inside rim of the pan, slightly overlapping the ends. Press them against the pan to form a smooth layer.

When the cake is cool, trim off the crust from the top, bottom, and sides. Cut the cake vertically into slices ½ inch (1.25 cm) thick. Arrange a layer of cake slices on the bottom of the pan, cutting pieces to fill the space completely. Drizzle half of the limoncello over the cake layer.

In a medium bowl, whisk together the ricotta and granulated sugar until well combined and smooth. Spread the ricotta cream evenly over the limoncello-soaked cake layer. Arrange another layer of cake slices on top and drizzle with the remaining limoncello. Cover with plastic wrap and refrigerate for at least 1 hour or overnight.

Invert the cake onto a serving plate. Carefully lift off the pan and peel away the plastic wrap.

Prepare the decoration: Sift half of the powdered sugar into a bowl. Stir in half of the lemon juice, breaking up any lumps. Sift the remaining sugar into the bowl and add the rest of the lemon juice, mixing until the icing is smooth and shiny with a thin, spreading consistency.

Spread the icing across the top of the cassata, leaving the marzipan sides visible. Decorate with whole and cut candied fruit. Refrigerate the cassata until set, 1 to 2 hours, before serving.

NOTES

- For a modern presentation and a fresh take, decorate the cassata with pomegranate seeds in place of the candied fruit.

- In place of commercial food coloring, a small amount of spinach puree can be used to tint the marzipan.

- The cassata can be made 1 day ahead and refrigerated until ready to serve.

WINE

SICILY'S RELATIONSHIP WITH WINE RUNS deep and strong. The Greeks arrived around 800 BCE, establishing colonies in Southern Italy, specifically in Calabria and Sicily, the so-called Magna Grecia. They introduced not only the drinking of wine but also the many social and symbolic rituals around its consumption, sparking a cultural revolution. In Sicily, the Greeks appreciated the island's rainbow of soil types—volcanic, sandy, clayish, limestone—that allowed for a great variety of viticulture. Additionally, with its diversity of altitudes and climates, harvesttime in Sicily can range from the end of July (for certain early white grapes in the southeast region) into November on Etna's slopes. Southern Italy has maintained an incredible quantity of centuries-old varieties and subvarieties of grapes, and those vines are witnesses to the most ancient winemaking practice we have.

When it comes to modern Sicilian wines, the story dates back to the eighteenth century. A storm at sea in 1773 brought the British trader John Woodhouse to Marsala, where he tasted the local wine produced there and enjoyed it so much that he exported hundreds of barrels to Britain, adding brandy to help preserve it during the sea voyage. Thus, Marsala, the fortified wine as we know it today, was born, and a large portion of the province of Trapani, including Mazara del Vallo, Partinico, and Alcamo, started cultivating vines to sell to Marsala producers. Woodhouse and his successors made such a fortune that they ended up lending money to the Kingdom of the Two Sicilies, which was formed when the Kingdom of Sicily merged with the Kingdom of Naples..

By the mid-1800s, Sicily had become the largest producer of grapes and bulk wine in Europe, most of it dark red wine that was high in both sugar and alcohol. In three decades, the cultivation of vines in Sicily doubled: In 1853, almost 360,000 acres (145,000 hectares) were cultivated. By 1884, that area had grown to almost 800,000 acres (322,000 hectares). By then, grapes were second only to wheat in Sicily.

Around this time, several Sicilian landowners started experimenting with indigenous grapes, as well as foreign varieties, and began bottling their wines (until then, most Sicilian winemakers had sold their product in barrels). French wines, especially Bordeaux, were the model at the time, and a number of enologists arrived from France. In 1824, Edoardo Alliata, Duke of Salaparuta, started his winery in Casteldaccia, not far from Palermo. Henri d'Orléans, son of the last king of France, established his prestigious winery in Carini, where he introduced French cultivars. Several other wineries also cropped up around Etna, Caltanissetta, Siracusa, and Mazara del Vallo. By the end of the 1880s, Etna wineries were producing red wine, Spumante-style sparkling wine, and brandy. Vines from Madeira and Bordeaux, as well as different varieties of Pedro Ximénez, were also imported and planted in Sicily.

By disseminating knowledge about careful farming and winemaking, these pioneers offered invaluable experience to the Sicilian wine industry. They began producing quality wines, which were bottled and exported all over Europe. This trend was just starting to gain momentum when, in 1879, the first Italian vine was affected by phylloxera, a parasite that attacks the vine's root system. Within a few decades, almost all European vines were destroyed. It was a huge environmental

disaster and, in Sicily, one of the triggers for a massive wave of emigration. (An exception was on Etna and in a few other areas where the volcanic soil proved to be hostile to phylloxera, allowing some old varieties to survive.)

It eventually became clear that the best solution was to graft Sicilian old-vine varieties onto American rootstock, which proved more resistant to the parasite than European varieties. This helped restart the wine and grape industry in various areas. The quality of Sicily's soil and its arid climate soon made the region the largest grape producer in Italy. The vineyards on Etna and in Alcamo, Marsala, and Vittoria started booming, producing huge quantities of grapes that were turned into high-alcohol wine sold in bulk to enrich lighter Northern Italian and French wines. But Sicily's focus on mass production meant that quantity trumped quality in many cases, a trend mirrored by the island's history of intensive crop farming, especially wheat.

This story started shifting around the 1970s and '80s, when government institutions, together with winemakers, began to encourage and support a different perspective on winemaking, with an eye toward making the best possible wines rather than the largest quantity. In 1980, Lucio Tasca started experimenting with international varieties, producing a Cabernet in 1989 that was a first for Sicily. Others followed suit. By the '90s, both local and foreign winemakers had come to understand the incredible potential of Sicilian soils and were eager to experiment with planting celebrity grapes such as Chardonnay, Syrah, Cabernet Sauvignon, Merlot … varieties that were untested on harsh, stony, clayish soils. The results were surprisingly good, and a star was born. Sicily gained international attention, and the world's perception of the island started changing.

Between 1990 and 2010, the number of commercial Sicilian wine producers grew from about three dozen to almost three hundred, and while some of those winemakers came from the Italian mainland or elsewhere in Europe, most were Sicilians who chose to invest and explore their own land. Around 2000, winemakers began setting aside international varieties in favor of more local grapes such as Grillo, Nero d'Avola, Zibibbo, Catarratto, and Nerello Mascalese.

Today, Nero d'Avola (for reds) and Grillo (for whites) are at the forefront of those cultivars. With its fruitiness, full-bodied aroma, and high alcohol content, Nero d'Avola long embodied the stereotype of Sicilian red wines. It became hugely popular around the world starting in the 1990s. Between 2000 and 2010, the number of Nero d'Avola vines planted increased by more than 45 percent. But recently, that type of full-bodied wine has ceded its place in the spotlight to more nuanced grapes, and growers are working on refining its potential. That said, Nero d'Avola is still the most popular variety grown in Sicily and is found everywhere on the island, with each area producing totally different notes.

Grillo, which was first documented in 1873, is a cross between Catarratto and Zibibbo and has become a flagship grape for northwestern Sicily. Its production has tripled since 2000, and it is protected like Nero d'Avola, meaning you can use its name on the label only within a Denominazione d'Origine Protetta, or DOP (in English, Protected Designation of Origin, or PDO).

Placing a greater emphasis on story and terroir, the wines from this new generation of educated and experimental winemakers represent the Italian wine avant-garde: the sweet and dry Malvasia from Aeolian vines, the Passito from Pantelleria, the Cerasuolo and Nero d'Avola from the southeast, and the bright minerality of Inzolia and Catarratto from the hilly central region. Inzolia, Perricone, and Zibibbo are just some of the many other "colors" Sicily has on its wine palette that are now gaining international fame and interest.

Winemakers now know that there is a world of difference between, say, a Nero d'Avola from the south born and raised on limestone and a Nero d'Avola from the center of the island born and raised on clay. This array of flavors is what matters, and this is what Sicilian winemakers want to celebrate, providing a more multifaceted and nuanced picture of Sicilian wine.

One can't talk about Sicilian wines these days without exploring Etna. Simultaneously destructive and creative, Etna has been the center of an inexplicable energy and power that have seduced and terrified Sicilians since the moment Homer's Ulysses and his men set foot on the island and tried to appease Polyphemus with a bottle of wine. The tallest volcano in Europe at 11,014 feet (3,320 m), Etna is now considered one of the top wine terroirs of the world. As wine historian Robert Camuto writes, the area has undergone "Italy's most dramatic wine renaissance. In the relatively short span of two decades, Etna wines have gone from forgotten—sold locally in plastic jugs or to tourists in tacky black bottles—to becoming the hip 'it' wines of the Italian South."

The volcanic soil found on Etna has a unique voice, one that has attracted a host of local and international players who have settled on its different slopes, each of which offers its own complexity and assets. The northern slope, crowded by vines that do not grow over 2,600 feet (800 m) above sea level, is renowned for well-structured red wines that can be enjoyed fresh or aged, notably Nerello Mascalese and Carricante. A different story happens on the eastern slope. Thanks to the breeze coming from the Ionian Sea, the vines can grow up to 3,300 feet (1,000 m) above sea level, plus there is more rain and wind, which allow for a wonderful growth of

Carricante and other white wine grapes. Milo, a small town on this side of the mountain, is the center for Etna Bianco Superiore, which requires this very specific type of soil, layered with volcanic sand and very few rocks. The wines produced here are refined and consistent.

The southwest slope of Etna is where you can read the full story of Sicilian winemaking, as told through the landscape of ancient trees, dry stone walls, small fields of unsupported vines known as *alberelli* ("small trees"), and gigantic millstones called palmenti. Here you can see and taste the past and the present, the pain and the wonders, the enthusiasm and the entrepreneurial skills of hundreds of farmers over hundreds of years.

RESOURCES

INGREDIENTS

Many of the Sicilian ingredients called for in this book are available at Italian markets or other specialty food shops. If you still need help locating a particular ingredient, here are some recommended sources and some of the items they offer.

BOB'S RED MILL
Widely available at local supermarkets
Chickpea flour, semolina flour

BUON ITALIA
Chelsea Market
75 Ninth Avenue
New York, NY
buonitalia.com
Dried wild oregano, pastas, semolina flour

DIPALO'S
200 Grand Street
New York, NY
212-226-1033
Sicilian cheeses, such as Ragusano DOP and Piacentino Ennese (in season)

EATALY
Various locations
eataly.com
Anchovies, capers in sea salt, pastas, Sicilian sea salt

FORMAGGIO KITCHEN
Various locations
formaggiokitchen.com
Sicilian cheeses, semolina flour, hand-rolled couscous, mosto cotto, pastas

GUSTIAMO
gustiamo.com
Bottarga, capers in sea salt, estratto, pastas, chickpea flour, semolina flour, Sicilian sea salt

MARKET HALL FOODS
Various locations in the San Francisco Bay Area
markethallfoods.com
Anchovies, bottarga, candied fruits, dried wild oregano

MILK STREET
store.177milkstreet.com
Candied citrus peel, chickpea flour, estratto

ZINGERMAN'S
422 Detroit Street
Ann Arbor, MI
zingermans.com
Modicana chocolate (Bonajuto)

EQUIPMENT

Very little special equipment is called for in this book. The few things that some may not readily have on hand are cannoli molds, a cassata pan (a deep-dish pie plate can be substituted), a couscoussiera, and a ridged board for making cavatelli (and gnocchi). All should be available at kitchen supply stores or online.

ACKNOWLEDGMENTS

Enza Di Gangi and Giovanna Di Bella are my two guardian angels, without whom the cooking school and most of these recipes would not exist.

Food expert Davide Puca thinks about food the way I do. His insight has been invaluable.

Ana Fernández and Henna Garrison are pillars of my team.

This book wouldn't be in your hands without my agent, David McCormick; publisher, Lia Ronnen; and editor, Judy Pray.

Kate Winslow and Guy Ambrosino are the best team I can dream of for sharing a culinary journey across Sicily.

Ivo Basile, Giulio Bruni, Giovanna Iacono, Giuseppe Cicero, Carlo Amodeo, Giacomo Gati, Agostino and Luisa Ninone, Erika Pino, Vito Impellizzeri, Mario Valenza, Emanuele Cottone, Stefania Barzini, Sandro Sangiorgi, Gabrielle Camiolo, and Filippo Privitera have all, in many different ways, inspired me.

And, of course, my husband, Gianni, who, together with Dillshan, Madu, Sadew, and Macchia, has ensured the right amount of peace and serenity around me to complete this book.

INDEX

FABRIZIA LANZA grew up as part of a renowned Sicilian winemaking family and has been immersed in the worlds of food and wine since birth. She studied in France and Northern Italy and worked as an art curator in the museum world for twenty-five years. In 2006, she returned to Sicily to help run her mother Anna Tasca Lanza's cooking school, where she continues to build on her mother's legacy. Lanza is the author of several books in both English and Italian, including *Olive: A Global History*, *Coming Home to Sicily*, and *Tenerumi*. She has also produced two short documentaries, *Amuri: The Sacred Flavors of Sicily* and *Amaro*. You can find her on Instagram at @fabrizialanza and @annatascalanza and read more at annatascalanza.com.